The Bali In Me

To Jeannie & Jim
and To "The Bali in
You!"

Dan
June '05

To order additional copies, please contact us.
BookSurge, LLC
www.booksurge.com
1-866-308-6235
orders@booksurge.com

DAN
PHILLIPS

THE BALI IN ME

A MEMOIR

Dandasana Books
www.danphillipswriter.com
email: dipmensch@aol.com

2005

THE BALI IN ME

To my loving wife and best editor, Judy, and to the people of Bali whose spirit and humanity made this book possible.

ACKNOWLEDGEMENTS

For their support and critique, Sarah Armstrong, Susan Maresco, Judy Slattum, I Madé Suryasa, T. Mike Walker, Melody Culver, and to Judy Phillips for so much more.

TABLE OF CONTENTS

PROLOGUE

In 1986, about to turn 50, I found myself smack in the middle of a mid-age crisis. My wife Judy and I were heading towards our 25th wedding anniversary. I received my Master's Degree in creative writing in the mid-1960s, aspiring to be a full-time writer; but married with two children, I took the more secure path to teach junior college English. Lately, my enjoyment of teaching began to flag along with my zest for life. I wanted to make a change in a more creative direction that would allow me to use my artistic talents, but how? Judy had made a success of her career in real estate; but she, too, wanted a fresh perspective to expand her artistic talents. We began looking for ways to celebrate this momentous year with an adventure that would renew us for another 25 to 50 years!

Judy Slattum, a former drama instructor at Cabrillo College whose improvisation class I took some years before, now conducted tours to Greece and Bali with her husband, I Madé Suryasa, the son of a Balinese Hindu priest. They offered an arts and culture tour to Bali, Indonesia that people testified as to having a lasting effect on their lives. We were intrigued, so we signed on.

When I stepped off the plane in Bali, I knew immediately why I had come. Magic was loose in the humid, sultry atmosphere like static electricity during a thunderstorm. People, dogs, insects, birds, palms, rice shoots, puffy clouds in the constant breeze, all were in motion. A symphony of sound surrounded me—the buzz of insects, the clang of a *gamelan* orchestra, chanting priests—all punctuated by coughing two-stroke motors.

These colliding sights, sounds and the myriad of impressions constantly streaming through my consciousness simply had to be recorded, so I started keeping a journal. My journals have multiplied and now form over a foot-high stack. They constitute a record in prose and poetry of seven trips out of which I have distilled the essence of my personal transformation. May it help you with yours!

Nehru called Bali
"the morning of the world,"
that place where we awake
to see ourselves anew.

I
DISCOVERY
First Trip—December 1986 through January 1987

From the moment we landed—on a sweltering afternoon in the middle of Bali's hottest, wettest season after a twenty hour flight, beginning in the middle of the night in San Francisco and ending two calendar days later—we knew we couldn't keep up our normal, Western pace. Stumbling out of the plane and across the steaming tarmac, we packed into the small, crowded and stifling pagoda-roofed reception hall. Following a weary search for our luggage, we joined a long line of tourists jabbering away in a polyglot of languages going through customs.

We piled into the waiting van and were immediately surrounded by a swarm of daredevil motorbikes and hordes of cars and trucks in the late afternoon rush hour traffic in Denpasar, the capital of south Bali. With no signs or white lines on the roads and few traffic lights, surprisingly, we saw no shaking of fists, blowing of horns or cursing.

On the roadsides, every inch of space was bursting with life. Women, carrying groceries on their heads, herding their children, exchanged pleasantries. Men, finished with their day's labors, sat at roadside stands having coffee, smoking and "schmoozing" or standing idle, viewing the passing scene. Someone was fixing a tire right next to people having coffee at an open-air café. Kids were playing soccer in the dirt between the cars and the foot traffic. The pellucid tropical twilight descended as we sped out of the city, following the contours of the hills and the sculpted rice field terraces towards the purple volcanoes in the distance. In every stream, people were bathing.

An hour later, we arrived in Ubud, the village which claimed to be the artistic and cultural center of Bali. Exhausted, we barely had the strength to tumble into bed.

Regrettably, the next morning did not seem like "the morning of the world." Sleeping fitfully in the muggy heat in the tiny room, we were jarred awake at dawn by bloodcurdling cries that ended in choking sounds. In the next compound, next street, next village, it seemed all the roosters on the island were bewailing their mutual fate at once!

Leaving our room, we found ourselves in a garden paradise in the middle of a rice field. While having breakfast on the open-air pavilion or *balé*, the charming owner, Madame Oka Wati, came by. "You are all *balé benggong*," she exclaimed. This, she said, was the Balinese way of just sitting and letting your mind go, thinking of nothing in particular. But that only proved to be a temporary state of mind.

After breakfast and a long walk through town to orient the tour group, Judy and I decided to take off on our own. Dodging aggressive motorbikers on the narrow footpath, we were soon drenched in sweat and dazed by heat. When we reached the road, Judy wanted to go one way and I another. Our argument soon became a source of entertainment for the gathering Balinese onlookers. Right then and there, we learned our first cultural lesson...

In Bali, land of balé benggong,
tourists must be peaceful in order to belong.

2

When we took our first excursion outside of Ubud to the Goa Lawah bat cave, it became shockingly clear how the Balinese actively maintain the peace, by balancing good and evil in their daily life.

Pulling into the parking lot, we were swarmed by scores of hawkers, shouting and thrusting their wares through the van windows. We made the hundred-yard dash to the temple as they tried to block our way. Adrenaline pumping, we were confronted with the gruesome sight of the large cave mouth in the side of a cliff, crawling with thousands of fat-bodied, hideously squeaking bats. The stink of guano was overpowering. Directly below the bats, beneath the cave overhang, was a simple Balinese temple encrusted with guano. We were told it was one of the holiest in Bali, directly related to the mother temple of Besakih, whose symbol of a dragon was chiseled into the stone altar. And there before it knelt our guide Surya, praying as peacefully as if he were alone in the forest!

Here at Goa Lawah,
we hang with the bats
between heaven and hell.

Time after time, I was impressed with how honorable the Balinese were. In the town of Klungkung, a young Balinese girl caught my attention, pointing to my wallet lying on the ground, having fallen out of my pocket. Then there was the driver whose aged van quit on him late one evening. He blamed it on "dirty gas" and persisted in the quick fix of blowing out the fuel line and pouring gas directly into the carburetor. We'd be on our way for a kilometer or two before the van broke down again. Finally, it could not be started no matter what he did, so he flagged down another driver, greased his palm with the rupiah meant for his own services, and ordered him to take us safely to our destination.

***

On our first day off from our busy tour schedule, we delivered a CARE package to a young Balinese girl my brother and his wife were benefitting who lived in the seaside village of Lebih, 9 km. away. It took two hours and three sweltering *bemo* rides with endless waiting in between at wide places in the roads, literally giant potholes filled with humanity instead of asphalt.

In 1986, the cheapest mass transportation in Bali was the *bemo*—a small, canvas-covered Suzuki truck with a rough wooden bench down either side on which as many people squeezed in as possible. You agreed on the price before you left and paid at the end of the ride. To get off, you either yelled "Stop!" or flicked a wire that activated a buzzer against bare metal which sounded like a giant bee caught in a jar. It's a wonder that the system worked and that you could extricate yourself in time from the tangle of humanity at the right place.

Riding a *bemo* was a true lesson in patience and humility. Bumping along on the narrow bench, Judy and I were somewhat embarrassed, since we took up enough room for four standard Balinese. All eyes were upon us. One little boy kept patting the hair on the back of my hands and arms with wonder as his friends laughed. Evidently, we were as exotic to them as they were to us.

Once we got to the little village of Lebih, we flashed our letter of introduction to the family in the neighborhood of Banjar Kesian. (All of Bali is organized into local associations called *banjars* that plan and oversee most of the social activities of each neighborhood for the welfare of the entire community.) After a lot of head scratching, we were led down a dusty road by an entourage of curious locals. As we entered the family compound, we were greeted by an older man, most probably the girl's father. He immediately climbed the nearest palm tree and returned with two coconuts, which he proceeded to whack open with his curved machete. Quickly and expertly, he gouged out holes in one end of each, inserted straws and handed them to us. Sipping our fresh coconut milk, we were ushered into a cement block building where we met Nyoman, the recipient of my brother's charity, the third in a family of four children. The pretty ten-year-old girl shyly shook our hands.

We were given seats of honor on folding chairs as ten children lined up in front of us. Relatives and neighbors quickly filled the small room. An old, toothless granny sat grinning in one corner surrounded by young mothers holding their babies. Those who couldn't get in peered through the glass louvered windows. Everyone was quiet as we quickly exhausted the few words we knew—*"Terima kasih banyak,"* "Thank you very much."

After an embarrassing silence, banging my chest and repeating the word "Phillips," I tried to explain that I represented my brother, the real benefactor. They all stared blankly at me. Wayan, the oldest boy, produced an old tattered dictionary where I found the word for brother, *adik*, but to this day I think that they believed the presents came from us and "Phillips" was the generic word for benefactor in English.

There was absolute silence as we began opening the large package. The young girl looked dazed and ecstatic as Judy handed her an American doll, a Mickey Mouse doll, school supplies—pens, pencils, crayons, scissors, notebooks. Then, to our surprise, Nyoman turned right around and distributed them to the other children.

Once again, we lapsed into silence. Then Judy, with the help of the dictionary, asked Nyoman to sing. Immediately, she burst into what sounded like the Indonesian national anthem. We recorded it on our portable tape recorder and asked the children to give their names one at a time. As I pointed to the first child in line, they all started shrieking at once while the adults appeared thunderstruck. I had forgotten our tour guide's warning that pointing with the finger was a taboo gesture meaning "penis!" *Ma'af ma'af,* "Excuse me!" I repeated many times over. Then, no doubt to relieve our embarrassment, they all burst into song. We applauded loudly and once more there was an awkward silence. What could we do now? In desperation, we sang "The Itsy, Bitsy Spider" replete with hand gestures which elicited loud applause. Taking advantage of this opportune time, we gathered up our things and made our way to the door...

We come bearing gifts
and leave enlightened
with more than we brought.

Everyone, with Nyoman and her family in the lead, followed us outside to the road. Fifteen minutes or so went by as we beamed good spirits at one another. In no hurry, we took off in the opposite direction from town to walk the few kilometers to the beach. They all just stood, watching us with puzzled expressions. We turned, waved goodbye, and they all waved back as we headed off down the road. Rice field workers waved to us from their shaded bamboo platforms, taking refuge from the broiling afternoon sun, as we passed...

THE BALI IN ME

Who can understand the tourist,
striding off in the afternoon heat,
not knowing or even caring where he goes?

The black sand beach was practically deserted. We had already heard that most Balinese would never think of going for a swim. They believe malevolent demons inhabit the ocean and most can't swim anyway. But down the beach from us, there was a small group of people in traditional dress watching some young boys swimming back to shore. One of the boys proudly held a live duck. Later we learned that this was part of the final act in the cremation ritual, when the deceased's ashes are scattered and a live duck is released into the water...

No need to feel abandoned.
When our souls are finally released
like the cremation duck,
we will be rescued
by laughing young boys.

We were surprised to see the brown, naked bodies of the duck pursuers, glistening with water, heading our way. Like so many sleek seals, they flopped down on the sand next to us. Chins propped up on hands, they watched our every move. One, completely fascinated, kept rubbing my hairy leg. Then two fully dressed teenagers joined us. Watching as we rubbed sun block onto our pink skins, they asked if they could also, laughing as they rubbed the goo onto their coffee-colored arms and faces. After we visited for a while, they accompanied us back to town and waited with us until the *bemo* arrived.

***

7

From the way the terraced rice fields were sculpted out of the hillsides, to the fine paintings and sculpture, down to the thousands of small intricately constructed banana leaf offerings we saw everywhere, it seemed that every man-made thing in Bali was done with an artistic touch. Our tour guides informed us that in Balinese there is no special word for artist, simply *tukang* or worker. Not only the numerous shopkeepers, woodcarvers, goldsmiths, silversmiths, jewelers, mask-makers, even the houseboy sweeping the walk in front of our room did his work with the care and consciousness of an artist.

The Balinese believe each artist has a *taksu* or special skill or talent he/she is born with. Balinese parents will often go to the *taksu* shrine at the family's temple to ask for blessings on their children to pursue their artistic talents. His or her *taksu* allows the Balinese, like any true artist, to see himself/herself merely as a vessel without the ego blocking the outpouring of the divine spirit.

My first *gamelan* concert took place on a perfect, sultry, starlit night at the pavilion of a local *banjar* or neighborhood association. Onstage, the intricately carved red and gold instruments were arranged in rows. In the rear were the large gongs, suspended from racks on either side of a large prop that represented a temple split-gate.

After everyone was seated, the players, dressed in white head scarves, yellow tunics and black sarongs, filed silently in and squatted cross-legged behind their instruments. Next, a white-robed priest came through the gate and sprinkled holy water on each of them as they closed their eyes and held out their hands to receive his blessing. Then he came down to the front of the stage where he knelt, sprinkled more water on a floral offering, lit the incense sticks embedded in it, then clasped his hands. A few minutes of silent prayer ensued, then the priest rose, bowed and left the stage. One of the two drummers on either side of the temple gate thwacked his two-headed drum, the great gong sounded, and the performance began...

Ever since I first heard
a Balinese gong struck,
my heart has reverberated
in time to the universe.

I was transported by the brilliant, shimmering, dissonant yet sweet sound of drums, cymbals, bronze pots and metal keyed instruments playing their complex, interlocking polyrhythmic patterns. After the opening instrumental overture, the lissome young dancers in their tight bodices and sarongs entered through the temple split-gate. No one seemed to be directing the drummers as they followed every nuance of the graceful dancers' movements...or were the dancers following them?

This question was answered poetically for me one day as we were walking down a street near the outskirts of Ubud. Judy S. pointed out to us that the Balinese were very proud of the roosters they train to fight and treat them with a great deal of care and respect. Their owners place them by the side of the road in loosely woven, lidded baskets so they cannot escape and may be entertained by the passing traffic...

Just as the Legong dancer's eyes dart
the instant the drum beats,
so do the rooster's inside the basket
when the car passes.

Included in the tour package were ten lessons from the Balinese master of our choice. After meeting four artists in their own home studios, each of a different discipline, I chose Agung Raka who was the leader of the Ubud *Gamelan Banjar Kelod*. His group had recently won honors as the best *gamelan* in the region and had just returned from a highly successful Japanese tour. Eight of us showed up that first day at the simple *balé* only a few yards from busy Monkey Forest Road, where the instruments sat under wraps out in the open on the bare pavilion floor.

I was filled with awe and anticipation as we lifted the canvas covers to reveal the intricately carved red and gold metallophones so deftly played the night before. Mallet in hand, Raka pounded out the five notes at the beginning of the *Baris*, or warrior, dance. When we started to play, he grabbed the mallet out of the hands of one of the ladies and shouted "No! not *nong nang ning nong neng...nang nong ning neng nong!*" and proceeded to bang out the notes again. It took our group of amateurs a full hour to learn the first eight beat phrase. But as soon as we did, his brow unfurrowed and his face broke into a big smile. *"Baik-baik...*good, good!"

The force of Raka's dedication impressed me just as the resonant, slightly dissonant, shimmering tones had struck a sympathetic vibration in my soul. I wanted to make that ethereal, meditative music part of my life. When we returned home to Santa Cruz, I joined a newly formed Balinese *gamelan* at the University of California with which I have been playing ever since.

A week or so later, winding our way down a mountain road towards the coast in the driving rain, we heard distant, bell-like tones. The driver stopped the van. There, in a gully just off the road, like an indelible watercolor which no amount of rain could wash out, a *gamelan* dressed in striking yellow outfits was enthusiastically playing away under a roofed *balé* witnessed only by two gigantic, ceremonially dressed puppets at least seven feet high standing on either side of the pavilion…

In the downpour,
players' yellow tunics
jungle greens
gamelan tones
all run together
for the pleasure of the gods.

Further along the tortuous, mountain road, we pulled off by a shrine. An old man leaned in the bus window, doused us with perfumed holy water and handed us flowers in return for a few hundred rupiah as a humble offering for our safety.

As befit the occasion, we wore our sarongs and sashes one night at a temple birthday celebration outside of Pengosekan, a village just a few kilometers from Ubud. The road was jammed with people in ceremonial dress crossing back and forth between the temple and the village square. Our driver found a place to park on a side road and hurried out. Every *balé* in the Pura Desa or main village temple which we passed was bedecked with flowers and elaborate offerings. We joined a crowd sitting cross-legged before a shrine. A young woman carefully placed a small pallet made from banana leaf that contained a bit of rice, some flowers and a stick of incense on the ground in front of us.

Surya showed us how to make our own prayer offering. When the priest rang his little bell to announce the time to pray, we lit our incense sticks and held flower petals between our clasped fingers overhead. Judy and I looked at each other and smiled. We had the same thought. Secular Jews who go to the synagogue during the High Holidays if at all, how could we ever imagine ourselves dressed like this, going through a sacred Hindu ritual? But it seemed perfectly natural...

The priest's bell has summoned us
many times before we can remember,
The splash of holy water awakens
us to our undying selves.

After this celebration, we drove to the nearby town of Batubulan for another temple birthday celebration. There we joined the village men gathered around the edges of a large, fluorescent-lit *balé* gabbing away, eating sticky rice cakes as long files of village women danced in unison the slow, stately, ages-old *pendet*. Each one, young or old, looked lovely in her tightly wrapped, lacy bodice or *kebaya*, ornately patterned sarong and gold-leaf headdress. I wondered if, in a past life, I could have first seen and fallen in love with my wife on just such an occasion?

Dancing the pendet
all women,
young and old,
Eastern and Western,
become one.

***

Near the end of our tour, we visited the village of Batuan where a cremation was in progress. We arrived at 11 a.m. to find the streets were already packed with people, since a well-known person had just died. Normally, the deceased is temporarily buried until the family raises enough money to afford a cremation ceremony, which can be quite costly. But since the person who had died was high caste and rich, he was being cremated right away inside a giant, ornate bull effigy.

For almost two hours, we were crowded against a stone wall in the gagging heat, besieged by hawkers plying the street leading to the cemetery where the actual cremation would take place. Finally, wrapped in a white shroud, the body was carried out of the house and placed inside a many-tiered *badé* or pagoda-roofed tower about fifteen feet tall that sat on a large platform made of thick bamboo poles.

With lots of enthusiastic shouting, more than a hundred young men lifted the pallet and tower and rushed madly down the street, spinning around and around as they went. The crowd, including us, surged to get out of the way of being trampled. It all took place in high spirits, with the bystanders laughing and dousing each other and the pallet bearers with paper cups full of water. A tourist videotaping the procession who got particularly close was showered and almost dropped his camera. Borne on its own pallet, the ceremonial bull (in which the body would be placed and eventually burned) followed the tower. Then came the clanging cymbals and banging drums of the marching *gamelan* with all of us spectators walking close behind.

We joined the procession to the cemetery where we passed another two hours sweating, leaning on tombstones, sitting on graves and waiting for the actual cremation to begin. A Japanese woman tourist fainted and was immediately attended to.

Finally, the body was set ablaze by acetylene torches. An intrepid woman in our group made her way to the front of the crowd to photograph this momentous event. The bull had completely burned away to reveal the shroud-wrapped body suspended inside. The moment it dropped into the inferno, she got her shot. Her curly red hair was indistinguishable from the swirls of flames which almost engulfed her as she kept on shooting. But the magic moment when the spirit departed could never be captured on film...

> *A flame burns inside us*
> *all our days*
> *and in the end,*
> *we are consumed by it.*

***

Just before we left Bali, we attended an all-night *wayang kulit* or shadow puppet play, at a birthday celebration for the Pura Desa in the woodcarving village of Mas just a few kilometers from Ubud. A light breeze showered us with silver moonlight streaming through the swaying palms. Here and there, kerosene lanterns lit up the shrines on which offerings were placed earlier in the day. After a full day of celebration, most older villagers returned to their homes, leaving a large group of children running about. We were as excited as they by the prospect of staying up late to see this magical show.

At eight o'clock, the scheduled time to begin, the shadowmaster or *dalang* had not yet arrived with his puppets, nor had the *gender wayan* music group that would accompany him. It began to drizzle, so we took refuge in a vacant *balé*.

The *balé* soon filled with excited, noisy kids casting curious sidelong glances at us. Here was a rare opportunity to observe exotic Westerners up close without being herded away by their parents. One little girl, about six, in a Mickey Mouse tee shirt and red skirt, squeezed in between my wife and I, gleefully smiling up at both of us. She pulled out a cellophane bag full of colored rice crackers, proceeded to tear it open with her healthy white teeth, then dangled it in front of me.

"*Terima kasih* ," I replied, "thank you," taking a few. Then she dangled it in front of Judy.

"*Tidak*," Judy, using her Indonesian to refuse, smiled back.

But the girl just shook the bag in Judy's face until finally she gave in and took a blue one.

"Mmmm...*baik-bagus*!" Judy said, "very good," making a face as she crunched away.

At least twenty children, closely watching the encounter, broke into hysterical laughter. Suddenly, there was that unmistakably vibrant, other-worldly sound of the ethereal *gender* instruments. The laughter stopped as the children immediately abandoned our *balé* and ran for the one where the performance was beginning.

We followed, breathing in the freshness of the light rain and stood while the children plunked themselves down on the moist ground in front of the stage. A sheet was suspended behind which sat four musicians in parallel rows of two each. In front of them and just behind the screen, the master *dalang* sat next to his box full of stiff, painted leather puppets ready to spring to life.

The *dalang* represents an age-old profession that passes from father to son. He is trained to perform for hours, manipulating scores of puppets that represent the entire universe of gods, demons and humans, while singing, chanting and talking in many voices and languages. As well as a healer and advisor, the *dalang* is considered a priest without whose presence no important temple ceremony can take place.

At the moment the *dalang* reached up to light the oil lamp

swinging above his head, the real world ceased to exist and the spirit world became illuminated. The scent of smoky oil combined with the cool moist air to make a heady concoction. First, the *dalang* displayed the complexly patterned, oval shaped tree of life. Then he quickly peopled his world with hordes of gods, demons, nobles and commoners while he recited the ancient story from the Hindu *Mahabharata*, making humorous asides in Balinese and slangy English. The children laughed, delighted as he made his puppets fly through the air and spring about on the ground as he chanted to the accompaniment of the silvery-toned *gender*. He accented the action and monologue by hitting his box with a piece of wood he held between the toes of one foot...

> *On the glowing screen*
> *the tree of life twirls and spins...*
> *gods and demons fight*
> *to possess our souls.*

It began to rain so the kids scrambled onto the covered *balé*, huddling around the *dalang* behind the screen. We stood in front under our umbrellas, equally spellbound. The shadow play was still going on a few hours later when we boarded the van for the short ride back to Ubud and made ready for our flight home...

> *Flying home, Bali becomes a shadow play*
> *flashing before my mind's eye.*
> *What was real, what imagined?*

***

After we arrived back in Santa Cruz, both Judy and I went into culture shock and hid out in our house for the next few days, not even answering the phone. I found myself deeply affected and spent much time meditating on what lessons I needed to learn from our Bali experience...

How to see my art as a necessary and joyful part of my life?

How to suspend my critical judgment, believe in the validity of magic and mystery and bring more spirituality into my daily life?

How to open myself to becoming a gentler, happier, more compassionate and loving human being?

How to preserve a sense of childlike playfulness, not take myself too seriously, and accept what I can't change in myself as well as in the world?

It might take years to live the answers to those questions, but now I realized I had the power to truly transform my life!

II
RETURN TO PARADISE
Second Trip—November through December 1991

In 1990, I joined the newly formed Balinese *gamelan* orchestra directed by Linda Burman-Hall at the University of California, Santa Cruz. It was named *Swarasanti* or "Sound of Peace" by our first of many visiting Balinese gurus or teachers, I Nyoman Sedana. Not long afterwards, Linda, Judy S. and I formed an exciting and unique organization that brought together "town and gown" to support the arts and culture of Bali in our community.

We called it Bali Banjar Santa Cruz. My Judy and I took our turn hosting a function at our home. Over fifty people attended, seated on our lawn as the *gamelan* played on the backyard deck. While I was hammering away on my metallophone, concentrating on a particular intricate and fast *kotekan* or rhythmic interlocking part, or ornamenting the melody on my flute, it didn't matter if I was thousands of miles away, I would instantly be transported to Bali...

Our home in California
has become a universal stage
where people can come together
to hear the "sound of peace."

The Bali Banjar Santa Cruz kept our interest in Bali piqued, and we began planning our return. In October of 1991, we took off on an extended trip through Southeast Asia including Thailand, Malaysia, Bali and the South Pacific. On this trip, we wanted to experience Bali village life without the support of a tour. Personally, I was most anxious to ground myself in a creative routine involving writing, music and the spiritual practice of answering those life-questions I had discovered on our first trip.

Just outside of Ubud, we rented a beautiful second story flat in the rice fields with a great view, open on all sides to the breezes. Our landlord was the genial, quiet and retiring Krinting, painter and husband of plump, jolly and most worldly-wise Wayan Klempun, a real-life counterpart of Bloody Mary in *South Pacific,* proprietor of one of the most popular restaurants in Bali, Café Wayan on Monkey Forest Road.

Judy and I were as surprised at them meeting our plane as they were to see us! We soon found out it was a case of mistaken identity. When I had talked with Krinting on the phone to reserve our lodging, he had thought we were their old friends, Don and Meg also from Santa Cruz, returning to Bali after many years' absence. After we all had a laugh, Wayan gave us both big hugs while the more reserved Krinting hung back, smiling quietly. From then on, I called her "girl friend" and she called me "Dan not Don!"

We were still laughing when we arrived at their restaurant, where we were treated to a glorious "rice table" dinner featuring the Balinese specialty, succulent smoked duck. Afterwards, we made our way home down a path into the rice fields under a starry sky to find big Madé, the night watchman, leaning against a post on the *balé,* half dozing. He jumped up to greet us and wish us *mempi manis*, sweet dreams, as he did every night thereafter.

Every day we were awakened by the pleasant but loud greeting of our houseman, Ketut, Wayan's younger brother, charging up the stairs with a pot of strong Balinese coffee followed by a tray loaded with bowls of delicious, sweet black rice with condensed milk and a plate of banana, jackfruit, pineapple and juicy mango...

In Bali, our night dreams are as sweet
as the tropical fruit we savor every morning
while the day stretches out before us
like the rice terraces to the distant volcanoes.

As we ate, we could hear the voices of the workers who had been in the rice fields since before dawn. A different phase of rice production was going on in each small rice field or *sawah* since the climate makes it possible to cultivate and harvest all year round. We watched some farmers standing in water over their ankles, thrusting the young shoots into the mud, and others straining behind their buffaloes and plowing or cutting down the rice with their scythes, just as they had done for centuries.

It was the beginning of the wet season. Most every night and many mornings it rained, and the air would be fresh and cool. One morning, over the sound of the plummeting rain, came some melodious strains. A rice field worker had taken refuge under our roof to play his flute. From the top of the stairs, I could just see his rolled-up pant leg caked with mud dangling off the edge of our *balé*. I didn't want to show myself for fear he would be embarrassed and stop, so I just listened and recorded his beautiful melodies on tape...

A fierce storm breaks upon us.
Rain drums on the thatch roof
while thunder cymbals crash.

A flute surrounds us
with sweet melody.
We are not afraid.

By ten o'clock, the rain stopped. Sweating in over 90% humidity, we couldn't wait to jump in the pool. Diving in, I experienced instant satori...

Hounded in the heat
by the demon torpor,
I plunge into a pool surrounded
by fierce guardian statues.
Emerging, I spy on the bent bodies
of rice farmers as they thrust
young rice shoots into the wet earth
while the gods watch over us all.

***

One day after breakfast, I was walking up the Monkey Forest road and heard the mellow, hypnotic sounds of the bamboo *tingklik*, a two octave xylophone-type instrument that consists of bamboo staves of various lengths tied together in a wooden frame, played by striking the keys with a rubber-tipped hammer. I had recently purchased one and was looking for a teacher. Eureka! Here was a crude sign on a board nailed to a rickety post that read "I Nyoman Warsa, instrument maker." A few yards away was a simple *balé* attached to a small, cement block house where a middle-aged man and a boy were playing.

I took a seat on the edge of the *balé* to watch and listen. Without any introduction, the man took his son's mallets away from him, handed them to me and said simply, "Now you play!" His son obediently and silently gave up his instrument. Being a complete novice, I tried futilely to imitate what he had been playing, and he burst out laughing.

With no further words spoken, I took my first lesson, haltingly, a note at a time. Every time I made a mistake, Warsa laughed and repeated the phrase. This went on for a good hour until I had had enough. He agreed I could come back for regular lessons. Then I asked him how much I owed for the lesson, and he laughed again. He finally accepted five thousand rupiah, a little more than three dollars. Warsa simply took it and responded "*besok*," or "tomorrow," then went back to playing with his son. "*Besok*," I repeated, and left.

I later found out that typically a guru doesn't ever ask for compensation. Payment is always slightly awkward, usually resolved by the student giving what he or she can afford as a gift. Three dollars became his usual fee, and he never once looked at the clock during my lessons.

Tingklik lessons became part of my daily routine. Every afternoon at 3:45, there would be the smiling Warsa waving to me from his *balé*. And every day I made mistakes and continually lost track of where I was in the bewildering cycle of patterns that made up each tune. Since I had never played the piano, it was difficult to isolate my hands and play a repetitive rhythmic figure with one while the other tapped out even the simplest of melodies. I stopped and started a million times. Every time I made a mistake, Warsa smiled, and, flustered,

I apologized. Then he laughed, having a good time at my expense. I soon realized that along with the *tingklik,* I was practicing the fine art of acceptance.

Warsa was never arrogant or patronizing. When I complimented him, he would humbly apologize for not being a good teacher. He didn't know English, so we hardly spoke, but he could intuit just what I wanted. He was sensitive to the smallest signs of my fatigue or impatience and allowed me the space to go at my own pace and try again—or, if I was totally frustrated, end the lesson. My progress was slow and painful, but I was learning.

One day, I was playing a simple tune involving both hands and enjoying the liberating feeling of not staring at the keys when there was an instant cloudburst followed by a deluge. Suddenly, I saw a sight that sent a shock down my spine, but I kept on playing...

> *Looking out at the slanting rain,*
> *I sit on my guru's bále playing*
> *as bare-chested men in sarongs run by*
> *carrying on their shoulders*
> *a corpse wrapped in a white sheet.*
> *This is my musician's dream*
> *to accompany my own funeral.*

Warsa explained that they were carrying the body of someone who had recently died to the cemetery at the nearby temple of the dead or Pura Dalem. This helter-skelter rush to bury the corpse was in stark contrast to the long drawn-out, elaborate and expensive cremation ceremony to ensure that the dead person would be reincarnated. For most people the ceremony would happen a year or so later, when the family had saved sufficient funds or pooled their resources with other families of deceased ones. Reincarnation was possible for anyone, including me...but would I return a wiser person?

Learning the rudiments and a few tunes was all I wanted, so after two weeks of lessons, I quit. On my final day, I bought some comic wind chimes from Warsa, which he kept outside on display. The Balinese equivalent of Punch and Judy, they became animated in argument when the wind blew and the chimes rang. Judy was chagrined to see how weathered they were, so we returned them.

Warsa was getting ready to perform his specialty, the *gender wayang* shadow play, for a cremation in another village. He politely listened to our complaint, although he seemed surprised. Nevertheless, he complied pleasantly with our request and exchanged the weather-worn wind chime for a good one, one of dozens of new ones he had stored in a back room. No matter that he hadn't given me a new one to begin with. We all laughed in good spirit. I purchased in addition an *angklung*, a set of bamboo rattles that sounded like the Balinese equivalent of Swiss bells when shaken. The wily musician might have sold me a drum if Judy hadn't put her foot down and said we didn't have any more room.

***

Enjoying long walks from our pastoral homestay on the outskirts of Ubud, one day we strolled to the town of Mas about 5 km. away, where some of the best mask makers in Bali lived and worked, stopping in art galleries and shops on the way with no intention of buying. Outside a new shop with freshly cemented walls, windows sparkling clean, a tall, thin man waved his arms furiously. We thought he was waving to someone driving by, but he kept it up. He was waving to us.

Crossing the busy thoroughfare, we were met by the owner, whose pleasure in having us as the very first visitors bordered on hysteria. He hovered over us, rubbing his hands as we perused the usual array of wooden Buddhas, Ramas, Sitas, Garudas and Ganeshas, Barongs, Rangdas, and animals of every shape and size. They were all priced higher than usual; however, we did admire a foot-high Rama and Sita clasping each other, bearing a price tag of 260,000 rupiah or about $80. Immediately, he grabbed it out of my hand and said, "Very beautiful, no? You buy!"

"What is your best price?" I asked.

He looked up in the air as if the answer floated there. When he met my gaze, his expression had turned quite serious.

"First customers. You buy, I have good karma. Please, what you pay?"

We were at that impasse where our motivation was really challenged. I looked at Judy, and she looked at me. Silently, we agreed that we really didn't want the piece.

"$20," I replied recklessly, hoping he'd stop.

Consulting his calculator, he smiled nervously.

"Sorry, too cheap...forty dollars, you take. Please, I must make good business."

He tried to force the statue into my hand. Again, I looked at Judy, and she looked at me.

I answered reluctantly, "I am sorry, too. We do not really want this."

Undaunted, he fired back, "Maybe you find something else?"

"No, *terima kasih*," I replied again, taking a deep breath. "I'm sorry, but we don't want to buy anything."

For a moment he looked dismayed, then he immediately perked up.

"Maybe later. First, you come to my village for special ceremony. My son one year. He get special name in six days. Here my card, Wayan Wesa. Give to your driver. All people know me!"

He pushed the card into my hand. We knew if we went, we'd be obligated to buy.

"I'm sorry we cannot come. We leave Bali very soon."

"Maybe you still come!" he replied, grinning.

Since we were leaving Bali in two weeks, I figured I could stall him out. I really didn't have the heart to say no.

"Maybe," I responded.

That was all he needed. He followed us to the door where he shook our hands vigorously.

"*Bagus*! You come. My family so happy to see you. We have special honor!"

Of course, we never planned to see Wesa again. But on the following Tuesday morning, six days later, as we were swimming in the pool at our homestay, there he was peeping out from behind the banana palms, gangly, grinning and dancing about like a crazed *jauk*, the mythological forest creature in a Balinese dance drama.

"*Selamat pagi!*" He greeted us as we paddled about. "I so happy you here. Now you go with me to my home for special ceremony!"

We had led the poor man on. As I pulled myself out of the pool, he crowded me so close, grabbing my hand, I couldn't help getting water on his sarong. I took a deep breath.

"I am sorry. We do not want to buy anything more before we leave," I articulated slowly, clearly and somewhat loudly.

His eyes froze, as did his smile. His nervous gyrations

ceased. Quickly, he turned and disappeared as if he were an evil adversary banished by a flick of the great god Rama's finger. We felt badly for leading him on. Did he think we were telling a story about leaving and decide to play on our guilt, figuring he had nothing to lose by taking another chance? Did we disgrace him by refusing to come to his celebration? At any rate, it was clear he had beat a hasty retreat to avoid an argument and possibly any further humiliation. We resolved in the future to be as sensitive as possible to avoid causing "loss of face," one of the worst things that can happen to a Balinese.

***

Thanksgiving arrived, and we were invited to a special feast at a restaurant owned by a Balinese man and an American woman. It was the real thing with yams, cranberry sauce, dressing, pumpkin pie and a tough little turkey. They don't run wild in Bali, and the Balinese don't usually raise them, so how they managed to grab a gobbler, we never knew.

There we met Bob, an early retiree from Alaska and Pam, a nurse from Seattle. We teamed up and hired Judy and my favorite driver, Kajeet, a soft-spoken, genial young man who was working his way through the university, supporting his new family. We asked him to take us on an adventure "off the beaten track." The next day we were off down a narrow country road, heading towards the mountains. We weren't gone fifteen minutes when we saw a lot of activity in a small village by the side of the road. The locals were preparing for the birthday celebration of their main village temple or Pura Desa. They invited us to join them in their activities, and soon Judy and Pam were busy with the women weaving strips of banana leaves to make the little pallets on which offerings to the gods and low spirits would be placed.

Bob and I joined the village men gathered around a heap of cutlery laid out on a *balé*. Squatting down with them, we hefted and appraised various items from the pile and jokingly began to bargain.

Before we knew it, we ended up with knives, heavy enough to be used as cleavers. With them, we joined the men kneeling at a long, wooden board, chattering away as they chopped up coconut, onions and long beans for a special festive dish called *lawar*. We were invited for lunch and sat down with the villagers to heaping bowls of a delicious chicken stew with crispy *krupuk* crackers and sticky, sweet rice cakes wrapped in banana leaves.

After lunch we politely excused ourselves, but they insisted we see their sacred Barong. This bug-eyed, large-toothed, fearsome tiger demon is beloved and worshipped by the Balinese. Every village in Bali has at least one of these sacred creatures who protects it from evil spirits. It was brought out of its special wooden cabinet in the village temple for the occasion and placed on the most prominent *balé*, festooned with flowers and many ornate multilayered offerings of fruit and whole roasted chickens held together by giant toothpicks. The next day the Barong would be paraded around to clear out the bad spirits and purify the village prior to the celebration.

We thanked them, and in high spirits took off again down the road. Soon we saw a man behind his water buffalo plowing up a muddy field preparing to plant his rice. Bob and I wondered what it would be like to plow, so we asked Kajeet to stop the van. I jumped out and slogged through the mud to greet the startled farmer. Why would a Western tourist make such a strange request? Nevertheless, when I mimicked plowing and pointed to myself, he offered the wooden plow handles.

The powerful buffalo lurched forward, nearly jerking the plow out of my hands, thankfully stopping or I might have pitched head first into the mud. With the farmer's help, I got a better grip and tried again. It was all I could do to keep my footing and hold on, much less keep the bit digging into the hard packed mud that came to my knees. After ten minutes with the farmer guiding me, I gave up, practically exhausted. He actually thanked me for helping him plow up his field! I thanked him and gave him 1,000 rupiah, which amazed him...

Hauled through the mud
by a beast who knows
his task better than I
as the rice farmer urges us on,
I bear down on the plow...
strain to cut into their world.

Bob did a better job since the mud didn't come up as far on him, but we couldn't help laughing at the tall, gangly guy stumbling along behind the big buffalo. I could just imagine what I looked like.

We paid a visit to the major district temple of Pura Luhur Batu Karu, almost hidden in a rain forest on the slopes of Mt. Batukau, "Coconut Mountain." To feel the power of one of the most ancient, sacred sites on Bali, I found an ideal place to meditate with a view of the surrounding, thick forest...

At Coconut Mountain temple,
on this stone step where no moss grows,
how many have sat here before me?

Afterwards, Kajeet led us to hot springs that poured into the river, cascading down the mountainside. There, we found rocks arranged to form small bathing pools. We eased into the hot pools adjacent to the rushing water, Bob and I in one and Judy and Pam in another.

Soon it began to rain. Completely immersed in hot water and conversation, we were completely unaware that the rocks that formed the pool were starting to disappear under the swiftly rising stream.

Suddenly Kajeet was yelling for us to get out *cepat-cepat*, "quick quick!" Luckily, we got out just as the last of the rocks were swept away by the torrent. In another moment, we would have gone with them!

On Batu Karu mountain
swept away by the peace,
we do not see the river
rising all around us.

***

Judy and I visited a village just outside of Ubud where a special ceremony of prayers and chanting to the Elephant God Ganesha took place to honor the ancestors. Three years before, Judy's father had had a debilitating stroke after a heart bypass operation which left him paralyzed, unable to talk, walk or care for himself. We knew he didn't have long to live, but now Judy felt her father's death was imminent...

It was a warm and sultry night on the open hilltop under the stars and a full moon. As our driver let us off, we could hear other-worldly chanting. Ghost-like images of people cast flickering shadows in the candle and kerosene light as we entered the temple grounds. We passed the stalls where sweet, sticky rice and all kinds of delicacies and trinkets were sold, moving towards the middle temple area where various ceremonies were in progress.

We were drawn to a pavilion filled with offerings and lit by scores of candles and clouds of incense swirling about the effigies of Ganesha. Many people, mostly women, were seated before the shrine where a white-robed priest sprinkled them with holy water. More of a wailing than a chanting, the women's voices welled up from the deepest recesses of their beings.

Judy sat down on the step of an adjoining *balé* and joined in with the worshippers...

At the temple festival under the full moon,
surrounded by candles and clouds of incense
before the flickering statue of Ganesha,
Balinese women wail for their ancestors,
my wife for her dying father.

Buying myself a sticky rice treat and a bottle of water, I wandered off to observe other groups praying and making offerings. I had an overwhelming feeling of *déjà vu*. Rejoining her, Judy told me that was exactly what she had felt! She had been communicating with her father. Reassuring him that she loved him, she encouraged him to stop struggling and let go. After she had chanted and cried with the other women, she was reconciled. A few weeks later in Fiji, we received word he had passed away!

***

Just before we left Bali, we visited a well-known and respected *dalang* puppet master who lived in the village of Bona. I Madé Sija had been the teacher of my friend and guru, Nyoman Sedana. Nyoman was now at Brown University studying for his M.A. He had urged me to visit Pak Sija and bring his personal greetings. Since Kajeet was booked, we hired a young, inexperienced but enthusiastic driver, Ketut. He fancied himself a tour guide and would turn around in his driver's seat to shout, "Attention please!" then jabber away in pidgin English about anything that came into his head he thought might interest us.

Off the main road, a village with dirt streets, Bona was from another century. Ketut had called ahead to make arrangements. God knows what he had said, for we were treated like long-lost relatives. As we entered his compound, Sija, a large, dignified man in late middle age with teeth stained red from betel nut, dressed in an antique sarong, got up from his rickety bamboo chair on the verandah to welcome us. I was struck by the intensity of his gaze as we shook hands. He introduced us to his oldest son, Wayan, who was attending Bali's College of the Arts or STSI, where he had been a fellow student with Sedana.

Sija wanted to hear all the news about Nyoman, whom he considered a second son. I taped his dramatic message to Sedana. As the recorder rolled, he addressed my guru friend as if he were right there on the verandah, sipping coffee.

A full-fledged *dalang* at age seven, Sija had been entertaining regularly on the average of three times a week ever since. He treated us to some beautiful chanting while his son played the music of the *wayang kulit* or shadow puppet play on a many-keyed, *gender* metallophone. Meanwhile his young grandson watched a show featuring Indonesian muppets on a TV suspended overhead from the porch rafters. What would happen to the precious and time-honored Balinese oral tradition soon to be in the care of this generation of Balinese children growing up with TV and computers?

Staring at the tube,
we cannot see who we are
or where we came from...
seduced by the black magic
of the electronic demon
who devours us.

Sija invited us to come back the following week for a special all-night performance of his *gamelan* that would take place at Bona's Pura Dalem or temple of the dead during the full moon: the *Calonarang* drama, a 16th-century tale of witchcraft and revenge involving the witch Rangda and her disciples. Rangda, the Balinese equivalent of the Indian goddess of death and destruction, Durga, is the warring opposite of the benevolent Barong. Her mask is absolutely terrifying with its bloodshot, bulging eyes, long, lolling tongue and wild hair. The performer becomes possessed as soon as he puts it on. I wanted to attend even though we were leaving Bali early the next day after the performance.

A week later, the night before we were scheduled to leave Bali, young Ketut showed up to take me (Judy chose to stay home and rest up for the trip home.) back to Bona along with his friend who drove. This left him free to regale me with nuggets of tourist info. As we approached Bona, Ketut became more and more agitated. It was twilight when we arrived, and he insisted on dropping me off at the edge of the graveyard, a few blocks away from the temple. Rolling his eyes, he said he never went into graveyards or even past them and especially wouldn't on such a dangerous night as this when all the low spirits were sure to be out in full force. But he promised to wait for me no matter how late it got.

I sauntered into the temple grounds where preparations were being made. Intricately woven, large, arching bamboo *penjors* were being hung and kerosene lanterns suspended from the branches of an enormous banyan tree overspreading the stage. A priest was chanting lugubriously over the loudspeaker. Sija introduced me to everyone as his honored guest, Pak Dan, using the Balinese term of respect for men who are heads of households. He explained that I also played in a *gamelan* in the United States and showed me to the best seat in the house, right in the middle of the orchestra that was slowly assembling.

Even though midnight was still three hours away, when the wicked witch Rangda was supposed to make her appearance, I could sense evil lurking there in the shadows of the large banyan tree at the edge of the stage. Meanwhile, *bondrés* or light, humorous entertainment was taking place. Clowns dressed in tatters of colored cloth pranced about, bare chested, mocking the vengeful mother of the *Calonarang* drama who had failed in her attempt to marry her son into royalty. The aged but still vain woman gyrated in her loose costume in a parody of a young, lithe Legong dancer. It was like being at the all-afternoon, Saturday matinee of my boyhood with serials and cartoons and a double feature.

Sija, the leader of the *gamelan* or *ugal*, struck his metallophone with all the energy of a young man. I was on the edge of my seat, transfixed by the brilliant *gamelan gong kebyar* exploding all around me.

Unfortunately, I couldn't give myself up fully to the night and the magic because of our early morning departure. I bid my farewell, waving to Pak Sija as he raised his curved, horn-shaped hammer about to strike his instrument. I caught the flash of a smile at me through his betel nut-stained teeth as he nodded.

Darkness surrounded me as I walked through the graveyard with only the full moon to light my way. Maniacal laughter came from the direction of the temple; perhaps the wicked, wild-eyed Rangda was chasing me! Quickening my pace, I tripped on a jagged gravestone, stumbled and almost fell...

There was my faithful driver curled up asleep on the front seat of the van behind the closed window. I called out, "Ketut, Ketut, it's me!"

"Whaaa!" he woke with a start, throwing up his hands. "Oh, it's you, Bapak Dan...I so glad you back!"

He thrust the door open, and I jumped in as he started up, grinding the gears in reverse to fling me back in my seat. Wheels spinning in the mud, the antiquated van coughed and rumbled, lurched off down the dirt road and back onto the pavement to make our escape...

Like a child on Halloween,
running through a graveyard,
I am pursued by demons
who will be chasing me
my whole life until I turn
and face them.

III
ART AND SOUL
Third Trip—July through August 1997

J udy discovered painting in an art process class she'd been attending for over a year. She had the brilliant idea of combining our next trip to Bali with one for her fellow artists. Along with Judy S. and her art teacher, Cathy Williams, she organized an "Art and Soul Tour." It quickly became a mother-daughter affair, with our daughter Caitlin making her first trip to Bali along with three other daughters of close friends. Nine women would be painting and touring Bali for two weeks.

After Caitlin left home and moved to Los Angeles a few years ago, I felt we'd lost contact even though we occasionally visited each other. I hoped that experiencing Bali would bring us closer together. But at the airport as we waited in the early hours of the morning to depart, every time I tried to share my enthusiasm, she excused herself and disappeared. When we queued up to board, I asked her why she was avoiding me. She whispered, "Cool it, Dad...just leave me alone, please!" "OK," I replied, but it put a damper on my spirits.

That first day, I awoke refreshed and went down to the pool at Ibu Oka Wati's while the artist group took off on an introductory walking tour of Ubud with Judy S. Writing in my journal, I was surprised at how easily I returned to that creative space I'd found in Bali six years before...

Let the day fall lightly like last night's rain
that barely disturbed the hibiscus petals.

Smiles break out as easily as the sun
from behind a cloud
whenever I meet Balinese eyes.

The banana paper absorbs the sweat from my hand
as the words flow from under my pen.

Impressions come when they come
like butterflies in the garden.

The second day, I planned to be gone by nine when the women artists would gather on our porch and set up their easels to paint. At eight o'clock, Judy shook me awake, groggy with a splitting headache. Jet lag had finally hit full force. Reluctantly, I pulled myself out of bed to gulp down the full pot of strong Balinese coffee our houseman had brought with breakfast…

In Bali, rice farmers
rise slowly before dawn
and are at work for hours
before tourists wake
in a rush to play all day.

I had hired a driver with van to whisk me away to the Art Center in Denpasar. The big annual Bali Arts Festival was taking place for three weeks, from the last week in June through the second week in July. There I met my guru and friend, Nyoman Sedana, now a teacher at the STSI and one of the official hosts at the Festival…

THE BALI IN ME

From all over Bali,
the masters have gathered
to make their musical offerings
to the gods and tourists
waiting to be entertained.

At the entrance to the *wantilan,* one of the large stages named for its large bamboo thatch roof, there he was grinning proudly in his multicolored sarong, sporting his name tag pinned to his blue Nehru jacket or *baju* .

After a morning of the best music and dance in Bali and touring the many shops at the Art Center, I ran into two more gurus who had taught and performed at UCSC with our *gamelan,* I Nyoman Sumandih and I Nyoman Rai, both of whom taught at the Bali College of the Arts.

After Sedana and I went out to lunch at a local *warung,* he invited me back to his home to meet his wife, Senih, and young child, Wina. Unfortunately, as soon as I walked in the door, I suffered an extreme attack of cramps. Breaking out in a sweat with a bad case of "Bali belly," I was more embarrassed than sick, but Nyoman and Senih were completely understanding and solicitous. Senih made a special yogurt drink to settle my stomach and offered me their bed to rest while Nyoman went back to work at the college.

Wallowing in the torpor of complete, disorienting helplessness, I lay most of the afternoon in that darkened room without windows listening to some roosters who sounded like they were being strangled as the TV blasted away in the next room...

You know you are home
if you enjoy getting sick
in a strange place.

A few days later, recovered, I joined the artist tour group for a trip up to the small mountain village of Munduk. There we stayed at the cooperatively run resort, Puri Lumbung or "rice barn palace." The resort is made up of cottages in the form of traditional, barrel-shaped rice barns set on piers high above the ground.

The rising cones of volcanoes carpeted with the lush coffee and clove plantations surrounded the resort. On the fourth side, each rice barn had an outdoor porch overlooking the spectacle of the purple mountains of West Bali that plummeted into the sparkling Java Sea. There, each morning Judy and I had our breakfast, and on the rice barn porch next door, daughter Caitlin had hers. Did she want her privacy or was she avoiding us?

Just down slope from the resort, we watched, framed against the rosy dawn, a rice farmer behind his water buffalo plowing up his small rice paddy. How did the poor farmer view us? Were we fat tourist chickens sitting in their rice barn cages, worth their weight in rupiah?

Following his ox, the farmer
bears down on the plow
as the sun rises.
Under his feet, the earth turns.

Man and beast went back and forth from one end of the flooded field to the other, and not once did the farmer look up from the earth in front of him. Was I projecting my guilt, deluding myself that I, the tourist-colonialist, should be the center of attention...for my daughter also? Were my expectations for her behavior keeping us apart?

THE BALI IN ME

I have a daughter
who has learned well
the lesson of her father
to follow her own light
while I stumble in the dark
and lose my way.

Back in Ubud, I invited Caitlin to accompany me to the Bali Arts Festival and meet Sedana's family. Instead, she chose to take a motorcycle ride with one of Oka Wati's houseboys to his nearby village. I was careful not to show my disappointment. The artist group was on a painting expedition to the women artists' cooperative, the Seniwati Gallery in downtown Ubud...

As I sit by the gate,
trying to still my mind,
Oka Wati kneels to make her offering.
Eyes closed, she wafts incense smoke
with her graceful hand
towards her slender body,
swaying as she prays.
Rising slowly, she leaves
without a word or sidelong glance.
Just then, a motorcycle roars up,
swerves to avoid me
and runs over the offering.
Madé, the driver, parks and
disappears inside the gate.
I collect the flower petals strewn about,
the bits of rice...
try to reassemble the offering,

then give up.
Now meditation comes easily.
I am at peace with myself.

Usually in their search for the few grains of rice, eager dogs and birds destroy the offerings as soon as they are made. The low spirits will not be angered since the proper respect has already been shown them. Just the gesture of making the offering is enough. Perhaps offering to be with my daughter, whether or not she accepted, was enough.

***

At the Arts Festival I rendezvoused with Sedana and his family at the large thatch-roofed *wantilan* to listen to the featured music from the district of Badung in South Bali. A reporter from the Denpasar paper, *Karya*, came over to interview me. Nyoman acted as translator.

After the preliminary questions, "What brings you to Bali?" "Have you visited here before?" he asked me if I felt the Balinese arts would survive. Nyoman encouraged me to be as candid as possible. I replied that, used properly, TV could be Bali's best friend, but if not, it could very well be the biggest threat to the survival of the arts in Bali. Bombarding the children with commercialism dulled them to the rich gifts they received directly from their family and community. I concluded by saying I hoped the younger generation, despite their predilection for things Western or American in particular, could keep their heads and their culture intact.

Nyoman agreed. That afternoon we returned to his home for a delicious home-cooked meal while his son watched TV. Sedana wants him to immerse himself in the arts and culture of Bali, follow in his father's footsteps and become a master puppeteer, a *dalang*. Like Nyoman, the Balinese believe they can benefit from exposure to the West, take what they need and still keep their own culture. I sincerely hope they are right.

***

The tour concluded, some of the artists prolonged their stay in Bali, most left for the States. Now it was family time. Judy and Caitlin planned to visit a spa and then join me in Munduk a few days later for the big, week-long, ten-year cremation ceremony.

The little village of Munduk buzzed with activity. Every ten years, the families pool their resources and share the cost and labor of an elaborate ceremony to cremate those who had died since the last cremation. For weeks, all over town, preparations were being made for the momentous event. On the side of the main road was the tall, tiered tower or *badé* containing the remains of the deceased that would be paraded along with the many black bull effigies under construction to the Pura Dalem or Temple of the Dead, a mile south of town, for the cremation ceremony.

Checking in at Puri Lumbung, I quickly unpacked and, dressed in my sarong, temple scarf and a festive shirt, meandered down to the Pura Desa.

In the outer courtyard, an enormous canvas tent was erected to receive the numerous relatives and guests who more than doubled the resident population. There the visitors and locals sat on folding chairs, partaking of coffee and sweet rice cakes and conversing loudly while a *gamelan angklung* provided a ceremonial background. Taking a chair, I was soon enjoying light conversation, mostly about who I was, where I was from and why I was here...

I am here to celebrate life and honor death,
to taste the bitter and sweet
of mountain coffee and sweet rice cakes.

From the tent, people circulated back and forth to another area in the middle courtyard of the temple. Above a long *balé*, paper decorations, artfully imitating palm fronds, hung from the rafters. Beneath the decorations were long tables with displays of photos, fresh flowers and smoking incense and what looked like fancy, upended hat boxes numbered from one through forty-seven, one for each of the deceased. These were stuffed with mementos like jewelry, pocket knives, photos and other personal items. Priests were blessing the mourners as they sat cross-legged before the ornate shrines, praying...

What would fill my cremation box,
my little life's legacy?

I wanted to take some photos of the worshippers and felt a little awkward until I was encouraged by one of the numerous priests dressed in white tunics and sarongs who busied about, overseeing the celebration. That night I slept well in the cool mountain air and awoke at dawn to watch the mists rising from the four peaks of Lesong, Sangyang, Pohen and Batukau...

Clouds lift from volcano peaks.
Sipping morning tea,
I awake slowly.

After a morning hike with Pak Gedé, the oldest guide at Puri Lumbung, through the lush valley between the volcanoes surrounding Munduk, I paid a visit to Pak Terip, the music director of Munduk, recognized as one of the premiere musicians in Bali. At the door to his concrete and stucco bungalow, I introduced myself by saying I was a friend of Pak Surya's. He nodded, but his face showed little expression, so I wasn't sure he understood. Without a word, he gestured for me to enter his large living room filled with *gamelan* instruments and have a seat next to him on a small carpet.

His wife silently served us some delicious Munduk coffee in fancy china cups that appeared to be the only luxury in this humble home. Seeing I had brought my Balinese flute with me, Terip gestured for me to play. After only a few notes, noticing I was having difficulty with some of the notes, he brusquely took the flute from me, pulled out his pocket knife and proceeded to work on it. First, he cut off the end to make it higher in pitch, then cleaned and filed the opening and adjusted the circular bamboo collar around it. Without a word, he handed it back. I found it worked much easier and better and had a great time playing together with Terip on his bamboo *tingklik.*

By the third day, Munduk was a small city, bustling with visiting traffic, and still the procession and cremation weren't for another few days. Surya arrived with his tour group, mostly seniors, all members of an outdoors adventure club from Portland. He invited me to join them for a long hike the next morning, and I gladly accepted.

That night I walked from the resort to town along the narrow volcanic ridge road bathed in full moonlight, looking up at more stars than I had ever seen and listening to the sweet sounds of a *gamelan* in the distance. Sure enough, when I arrived at the village temple, a small *gamelan anklung* was gathered alongside the pavilion where the mementos of the dead ones were kept. I took a seat on a stone step in front of the *gamelan...*

In a swaying sea of serious young men
in blue Nehru jackets,
that old, grinning, toothless guy,
dressed completely in white,
bobbing up and down and
pounding away with his mallet is me!

It had been ten years since our first trip to Bali, about the same time as the last Munduk cremation. A cycle in my life had been completed, and I was ready for another to begin.

I wrote in my journal...

I feel I have to let something go for my artistic spirit to be liberated--make some sacrifice. Could the sacrifice be my ego?

The next evening when Caitlin and Judy arrived, we heard some visiting musical groups and Pak Terip's local *gong kebyar*, resplendent in their yellow jackets and black sarongs. The villagers crowded in on all four sides of a square of canvas laid right on the ground, as two young girls danced the *Panyabrama* or welcoming dance. Then a tall, graceful American girl, Sasha Friedlander, from our hometown of Santa Cruz, performed the difficult and artful *Legong*. The Balinese stood slack-jawed as they watched this accomplished young American girl dance...

For thousands of years, young girls
have skillfully danced barefoot on the earth
before they become women.
And, on this magic, tropical night,
it is easy to understand
why this young, white American
believes she was Balinese in a past life.

Taller than the awestruck, adult villagers
who surround her, she bends delicately
in her tight bodice. Palms arched,
fingers trembling, she weaves
a tapestry, intricate as a double ikat,
dancing the Legong
on a square of torn canvas.

Soon this same girl will return home to California
to swing dance, ponytail and skirt swirling,
on a polished high school gym floor...
already a goddess.

Watching Sasha's mother, Sara, beaming proudly and her father, Cliff, record this rare event with his video camera, I realized how much I appreciated my own daughter.

The next morning, we awoke to loudspeakers blaring away. We had a quick breakfast, put on our finest sarongs and temple scarves. I donned my special white and gold embroidered headband. With our cameras, water bottles and tape recorder, we hustled down to the village where the procession was forming. Nine o'clock and already the sun was burning hot. The main street that headed down the long, narrow volcanic ridge towards the sparkling Java Sea in the distance was jammed with people in ceremonial dress. Horns beeping, vehicles were slowly making their way through the crowd.

By the side of the road, across from the grounds of the temple, the priests in white tunics were carefully transferring the large bundles of the deceased's effects up a gangplank and into the tall, *bade* tower with its eleven pagoda roofs or *merus*. Although they might contain the bones of the dead, the bundles' contents were mostly relics. Each one was wrapped in white cloth and marked with an identification number. Two men, dressed in antique warrior costumes and brandishing broadswords menacingly, ran up and down the gangplank, no doubt to ward off the evil spirits. Delivered to the Temple of the Dead, the bundles would eventually be placed inside the large, black bull effigies and cremated.

It took a good hour to transfer the 47 bundles, one at a time, from the temple into the *badé*. We took refuge from the sun under an overhang in front of the town marketplace, attracting more attention than the spectacle. Balinese bystanders queried us, anxious to use the little English they knew. Where were we from? Why had we come? A little girl pulled on my sarong, almost undoing it. As I secured it tighter, I drew laughter from the Balinese as well as Judy and Caitlin.

The last of the bundles loaded in, there was a shout, and twenty husky young men lifted the *badé*, on its pallet of crisscrossed, thick bamboo staves, onto their shoulders and began their fast pace down the road. Unlike a Western funeral procession, everyone was enjoying themselves tremendously. On the sidelines, people were laughing and shouting, hurling cups of water at the sweating men as they passed.

The parade was led by a man, jerking and weaving about as if in a trance. Naked to the waist, he brandished a stick with the effigy of a pig stuck on it. He was followed by giant, comic papier-mâché dummies of a man and a woman wearing spectacles, then scores of women, each in her colorful sarong and lace *kebaya* and carrying elaborate offerings on her head. After them came the exciting *gamelan beleganjur*, metal pots tinkling hypnotically, cymbals crashing, led by Pak Terip, his hands a blur as he beat his two-headed drum.

Along with the villagers and visitors, we fell in line behind the *gamelan* for a long, slow walk under the broiling sun, down the ridge to the Pura Dalem where the cremation was to take place. On the way, we stopped at a large metal, shed-roofed structure where young men and women were having their faces made up, along with last minute adjustments to their elaborate, gold-embroidered costumes. The women wore gold crowns on their elaborately coifed heads, lace *kebaya* blouse-jackets and sarongs. The bare-chested young men, swords slung across their backs, wore fancy embroidered sarongs and gold-embroidered headbands. As we passed, the young men and women joined the procession in a stunning display of beauty.

It was mid-afternoon when we finally arrived at the Temple of the Dead. Over a thousand people were spread out on a hillside overlooking north Bali and the sea beyond. The large *badé* had been placed in proximity to the bulls. As the loudspeaker droned interminably, announcing the deceased by their numbers, white robed priests preceded by the antique warriors waving their swords, removed the bundles one at a time, carried them down the gangplank and placed them inside the bulls...

Clouds spin across the sky
The loud speaker sputters...
Today 47 souls depart for paradise!

***

After the cremation, a taxi took Judy, Caitlin and I to a seaside resort in Pemuteran on the northwest coast. There we snorkeled off nearby Menjangan Island, where the shallow sea washes over a reef extending some twenty yards out from the shoreline where it suddenly drops off to a depth of over a hundred feet.

We allowed the gentle current to take us around the steep sea wall out of which popped fish of every color and type within effortless reach. They swarmed around us like we were fellow denizens of the deep as we took turns snapping pictures of ourselves with our underwater, throw-away camera. Back at the resort on Pemuteran Bay, Taman Sari, we dined under the stars and afterwards were lulled to sleep by the sounds of the gentle surf.

Caitlin slept like a princess on an outdoor bed covered by mosquito netting that appeared to be floating in the middle of a pond with flowering lotus pads. Coming into our room as we were having our coffee the next morning, she took a stool across the breakfast bar from us and regarded us coyly. "Good morning, parents…I had a good night's sleep and a great dream."

"What about?" Mama Judy asked.

"Oh," she propped her chin on her crossed palms, "being home with you guys again. Dad making me drink fresh squeezed orange juice every morning."

We all laughed.

"You're lucky we're in Bali," I replied.

Her gray-green eyes turned serious.

"You've given me more than orange juice, Dad. You too, Mom…You've both given me a glimpse into a life dedicated to the spirit by bringing me to Bali."

She took a sip of juice and peered over the rim of the glass directly at me.

"I just had to experience it for myself, that's all."

"I understand," I replied.

Then she reached over and touched my hand.

"I've never felt closer to you, Dad."

My daughter and I
had to travel thousands of miles
to find how close we really are…
two souls on a holy mission
to discover ourselves.

A few days later, we all said our sweet goodbyes at the road where our driver, Dewa, waited to take Caitlin to the airport. Once again, she thanked us for her Bali experience and resolved to come back soon.

***

While we were in Pemuteran, four members of our UCSC Balinese *gamelan* had arrived in Ubud along with our director, Linda Burman-Hall. She rented a set of instruments, and we rehearsed afternoons at her home in Ubud, an idyllic setting on her terrace patio overlooking a jungle stream…

Notes pour from our gamelan,
float into the cosmos.

Commuting from Denpasar, Nyoman Sedana joined us to teach us a new piece. We also rehearsed a piece Linda discovered in the Library of Congress. We planned a performance in the village where the piece had originated thirty-six years previously.

I had other enriching musical experiences. A young musician named Koman from the nearby village of Mas, who performed with the famous Ubud group Semara Dana, taught me the complicated flute part of their signature piece, *Semara Ratih.*

Judy and I went to the new Jazz Café in Ubud to hear an Indonesian trio with a Javanese woman who sounded like Billy Holiday. At the break, I introduced myself, and she invited me to join them for the next set on clarinet. A week later, I returned and played a few numbers with an alto sax player from Australia. The next day on the street, someone who had been there stopped to congratulate me. Overnight, I had become a Bali jazz star!

Playing music in Bali
I repay the gift of the spirit.

***

Our time in Bali was fast slipping away. Nyoman and his family braved the Denpasar rush hour traffic on a motorbike to pay us a goodbye visit. Nyoman was in the driver's seat, young son Wina squeezed in between him and the handlebars. Senih, his wife, hung on from behind.

After lunch at Oka Wati's restaurant, we were due for a rehearsal at Linda Burman-Hall's, but Sedana wanted to swim first. He called me his swimming guru. Three years before, I gave him his first lesson in Santa Cruz. When he apologized for not practicing, I assured him I had no expectations and was happy just to teach him something in return for all that he had taught me. We exchanged small gifts, a blouse for Senih, a tee shirt for Nyoman who brought me a startling, bug-eyed, forest demon or *jauk* mask he had used to perform. Meanwhile, little Wina turned out scads of spontaneous crayon pictures for us at the table on the front porch.

The next morning, I awoke stimulated and anxious to make the most of the remaining days in Bali...

Frangipani scents the air
fresh from last night's rain
when my young guru visited.

Judy and I celebrated the spirit on a misty day at the mother temple, Besakih, on the slopes of Mt. Genung Agung, which is really a complex of temples. The priest who cared for the temple called Ganeg, devoted to prosperity, led us through the steps in becoming blessed. With bits of rice stuck to our foreheads, a sign we had been received by the gods, we lifted flower petals overhead and prayed for world peace and understanding to all three Gods of the Hindu trinity: a red petal for Brahma, a white one for Wisnu and a blue one for Siwa. The jagged summit of Genung Agung appeared from behind the clouds which continually surround it. Our prayers had been answered.

The next morning at poolside, we heard the rumble of drums and the clanging of cymbals of a cremation procession in progress in downtown Ubud. The pool quickly emptied out as the tourists scampered to get dressed while we continued to sip our pineapple juice.

Then there was a moment of silence as a couple of doves cooed to each other across the rice paddy. I felt a shiver down my spine. I picked up my journal and wrote the stanzas I needed to complete the long poem I had been working on for the duration of this trip.

Here is the final version I finished some years later...

Frangipani scents the air
fresh from last night's rain.
Sipping morning tea
I awake slowly.

Suddenly drums rumble
cymbals crash
gamelans clang
dogs howl
tourists run...
The cremation has begun.

Why rush?
For years the dead ones
have waited patiently
to be released,
and at their leisure,
the gods descend the incense trail
to partake of lavish offerings.

Following the ox, the farmer
bears down on the plow.
Between his legs, the earth turns.

Clouds spin across the sky
The loudspeaker sputters...
47 souls depart for paradise.

A dove calls to its mate
across the rice paddy
I am no longer here.

As we winged our way homeward, I conceived the idea of a book based on my journals with prose and poetry. If I never had another opportunity to return, at least I would have the book.

Little did Judy and I know that we would soon have a home in Bali, guaranteeing many more visits and enabling us to make some big changes in our lives.

IV
SPIRITUAL RENEWAL
Fourth Trip—March through April 2000

Following my 60th birthday, I longed for a renewal of the spirit. Retiring from teaching in June of 1999, now I could fulfill my lifelong ambition to devote myself to the arts. In a burst of creative energy, I was playing in three different music groups, working on a book of poetry, a screenplay and this book. Anything was possible. My spirit was expanding.

In the summer of 1999, we received a momentous email from our friends, Judy and Surya, who were on tour in Bali. They were in the process of purchasing a garden compound with two homes in the countryside near Ubud and were looking for partners. Did we want to go in with them and take one of the homes?

We were tremendously excited and ready to accept, but was it practical? My Judy was still working, and we both had commitments in Santa Cruz. We would only be able to visit sporadically. And what about maintaining a property 6,000 miles away that, according to Surya, required extensive renovation?

On the plus side, Judy and Surya would be there half the year to oversee the property. Not only would we have our own place to stay when we visited, but we could rent it or exchange it with people for their homes anywhere in the world! It would be a big responsibility but well worth it. We emailed back, "We want it!"

Judy and Surya returned to California with a video of the three-quarter-acre terraced compound. Stone walls enclosed lush gardens, ponds and two beautiful Balinese and Javanese style homes. On the video, Surya repeatedly intoned the words "all teakwood" as he panned the camera over the 150-year-old, Javanese nobleman's home. It had been taken apart in Java, transported to Bali and reconstructed on the upper terrace by the compound's former German owner and his Javanese wife.

We worked on an agreement spelling out the terms of the lease-purchase. In exchange for a reasonable sum, we would receive our home in good structural and functional condition. After that, we would make any improvements at our own expense. We would own the house outright and lease the portion of land on which it was situated from Surya, the official landowner, for a period of twenty years with the option to renew. Besides sharing in the costs of maintenance and the household staff, we would participate in grounds and site improvements. On November 3, 1999, the die was cast! We signed and paid our share in full.

Besides adding a new bathroom and kitchen, much had to be repaired or replaced since the house had been neglected for three years. We were hopeful the renovation would be complete by March of 2000 when we planned to visit again.

Judy and I looked for signs that we had made the right decision. Just before we left for Bali, I took a walk on the seashore early one spring morning, the surf surging over my feet, and experienced a wonderful sense of well being. If I died tomorrow, I'd be completely satisfied...

My life is like...
a gamelan, ringing the changes,
or a Bali sunset,
with flashes of insight
followed by an afterglow of wonder.

How could I have known I'd be feeling so vigorous and full of adventure at 62?

According to Surya, who was at that time in Bali, our compound had been blessed by the local priest and the work was progressing but might not be completed when we arrived. So we made reservations at Oka Wati's, where we had stayed in '86. Once landed, we headed directly from the airport to the mountain village of Munduk to rest up from the long flight.

There we learned from Surya that he had to fire the workers. They had not done their job, and the kitchen and bathroom were still not in. He was having a difficult time finding skilled *tukang* to replace them. Although disappointed, we were reconciled to visiting and watching the progress in hopes that the place would be finished during our stay in Bali.

***

That first morning, we sat on the verandah of our mountain cabin watching the sun rise over the sloping green-carpeted volcanoes...

Early March...
Rains have ceased.
Green slopes of volcanoes
tall clove trees
bushes of red-berried coffee

all emerge from the mist.
Stories of ancestors are told
in the patchwork of rice paddies
punctuated by the terra cotta roofs
of stone houses…

350 years ago, people arrived from Tabanan
after the great empire of Gegel had collapsed.
Poor and homeless, they were given land
and a new life by good King Gusti Sakti.

Now, from across the ocean
we have come starving
from having too much,
hungry for enlightenment.

Suffering jet lag and the sudden temperature drop in the mountains, we booked massages that first night from Pak Suwitra, a shaman well known as the local healer. Spectrally thin and wild-eyed, he showed up at the door around nine. Judy was first, lying on her stomach in bed. Suwitra motioned me to a chair next to the bed. Then he climbed right on top of her and without a word began leaning on her back with all his weight. She let out a little cry of surprise which he quickly drowned in a gruff but friendly Balinese babble that he kept up for the next two hours, an hour for each of us. Every once in a while he'd say "strong strong…good good…or no strong, no good," as he manipulated a leg or an arm. In return, we'd babble away in English, and he nodded as if he understood every word. When he was through, he took his money and disappeared without a word into the cool, starry mountain night. Had we dreamt he had been there?

Suwitra's magic worked. After three days of hiking and relaxing in beautiful Munduk, we felt ready for Ubud. We couldn't wait, anxious to participate in the renovation of our new home and watch it being transformed.

***

Ubud had changed. The days of being able to take a stroll down the Monkey Forest Road and watch the ducks waddle over the rice terraces in pursuit of tasty insects on the young rice shoots were gone. Now shops catering to tourists were jammed, chock-a-block down the length of the busy road.

After a scenic five kilometer ride, with Surya directing the driver through the countryside south of Ubud to the village of Lod Tunduh, the van came to a halt next to a large art gallery. An elephant statue marked the entrance to the narrow *gang* or path that led by the wall surrounding the gallery and past a simple compound and a pen, where a large mother pig was lying on her side while a host of babies nursed. My heartbeat increased as we took a sharp turn into the placid rice fields where a beautifully sculptured shrine to the rice goddess Dewi Sri stood, past small, delicate cows grazing. At the end of the path was a moss-covered, stone-arched gate with its wooden door wide open to greet us...

Entering the gate to our Bali home,
we step across the threshold into our dreams.

Surya went in first. Smiling, he beckoned us inside. Judy and I closed our eyes, joined hands and entered. And there it was as we had imagined, only twice as spectacular! From its windowed peak, the pagoda-style tile roof sloped down equally on all four sides, overhanging the carved teakwood and glass sliding panel doors that stood open to the breeze. In front was a lotus-covered pond surrounded by a lush garden. Holding my breath, I stepped across the pond that encircled the house (which Surya assured us would soon be filled with water, lily pads, reeds and, of course, frogs) and into the large, open room.

In the exact center was a *balé.* "All teakwood!" Surya laughingly mimicked his video pronouncement. Above it, supported by four posts, stood a canopy made of ornately carved, teakwood framed panels. Surya explained that this was the portion of the house that gave the *joglo* its name. Apparently, after the German owner died, his Javanese widow had been offered a good sum of money just for the canopy, which was supposedly museum quality. Lucky for us, she had refused. I climbed the wooden ladder above the canopy and found in the garret, to my surprise, a small loft with a teakwood sleeping platform and windows looking out on the entire compound and the surrounding countryside.

We crossed through the breezeway created by the abutting roofs of the *joglo* and the shed roof of a new stone building adjacent and found two dark, dank, empty rooms. We discussed turning one of the rooms into a kitchen and the other, from which steps led to an unfinished open-air, Balinese-style bathroom on the terrace, into a bedroom. Surya planned to partially enclose the bathroom with a semicircular wall, extending the portion of the roof that covered the toilet and wash basin over the slate-lined bathtub.

It was a beautiful property but needed much basic work. There was no plumbing and electricity. Repairs to make up for the years of neglect had to be made. Rot from the torrential rains had taken its toll on the roof and walls. Termites were in the foundation and, in many places, had eaten away the floorboards.

The work was proceeding at a snail's pace. On our next visit, we found an old man, who could hardly bend over, taking great pains to measure a rotted beam to be replaced as his young son watched closely over his shoulder. No work on the kitchen and bathroom had been started. A few days later, Surya informed us that he had to let the man and his son go and hire an architect/contractor to get on with the remodel. Surya, his brother Gedé and brother-in-law to be, Agus, had spent months working on the other house where Surya and Judy would live. Also, there was a great deal of landscaping and gardening to be done. But this, after all, was Bali, where everything took place in *jam karet* or "rubber time"…

Time is rubber
as we bounce along,
roll with the earth
around the universe
of our desires.

The Indonesians had to have time to purge themselves from the old corruption of the Suharto regime, and the entire world had to take time to cleanse itself of countless sins against the environment and the poor and disenfranchised. It was fitting that the New Year's holiday of *Nyepi* was coming on April 4, when the entire island would undergo a ritual-filled purification.

From the moment we got off the plane, we had been aware of preparations being made for the big holiday. Every town and neighborhood we passed through displayed a giant, fanciful dummy under construction made from bamboo, wire, styrofoam, papier mâché, any material possible. When completed, these towering monsters called *ogoh-ogoh* with their bug eyes and claws would be stationed at prominent intersections and then paraded about, the day before *Nyepi*, to ward off the evil spirits.

All over the island, we saw teenagers having a great time constructing the particular, devilishly imaginative demon that would represent their neighborhood. One scary, hairy behemoth at least ten feet high with extended six-inch claws stood at a *balé banjar* on Monkey Forest Road next to the soccer field, just a few blocks from Oka Wati's. Over the course of three weeks, we watched as its bamboo frame slowly disappeared under a papier mâché covering coated with dried, stringy thatch.

The teenage builders roared with laughter when Judy directed me to stand right under the claws of the beast for a snapshot...

> *I turn my back on a dummy*
> *reaching out its claws,*
> *towering over me,*
> *an even scarier, tourist monster*
> *who grabs anything he wants.*

In the week prior to Nyepi, every Balinese community and individual would undergo purification with prayers, ceremonies and processions to the sea, or the nearest body of water, to make offerings and receive blessings from the priests. On *Nyepi* eve, the best of the *ogoh-ogoh* from all over Bali would be paraded down the middle of Denpasar to compete for prizes. Surya and Judy invited us, along with their tour group, to that huge, wild Balinese New Year's party.

Nyepi day would be just the opposite. From dawn through the next evening, everyone would remain in their family compounds to meditate on their past sins and purify themselves in preparation for the New Year. Imagine a whole day of silence! No one on the streets, no coughing motorbikes, blaring horns, roaring cars, trucks or airplanes. All Bali would be quiet and observant. What a way to bring in the first year of the New Millennium!

***

We might not be able to move in, but we could decorate and personalize our new home. The week after we arrived in Ubud, we embarked on an expedition to look at furniture. We visited a few rattan and bamboo factory showrooms and purchased some pieces but, in the end, decided to buy mostly classic Javanese style teak and mahogany that suited the style of our antique *joglo*.

A friend from Santa Cruz recommended someone with a furniture business in Kuta-Legian...

Gridlock in the center of Denpasar,
as evil threatens to overturn good.
Bound for honky-tonk Kuta
where anything can be had cheap
to furnish our new home in the rice fields,
our van is ensnarled in traffic circling
the feet of gigantic stone gods locked in combat.

Our driver informs us
his parents died of cancer and stroke.
Overweight and sedentary, he worries
he shares the same karma.

As he threads our way
out of the jammed roundabout,
we advise not to eat foods fried in coconut oil
and get a good exercise regime...
while we all continue to breathe
the toxic exhaust of creeping capitalism.

Irrepressible Mari, a petite and dynamic Javanese bundle of energy, seemed to know exactly what we wanted. After we made our purchases, she offered to come out to the *joglo* to help us with the decor, suggest other items we might need and consult with us on the wiring and fixtures which we could purchase at wholesale prices through her.

***

The wedding of Ketut Suryani, Surya's lovely sister, was to take place at the family home in Denpasar. She was marrying Agus, a trained veterinarian who planned to open his own practice with the proceeds of a thriving bean sprout business in the Ubud marketplace. In accordance with tradition, Ketut would come to live with Agus in his family home.

The night before the wedding, I had a dream about my father. I was a baby and he was bending over my crib, smiling as he snapped my photo. We had never been close. Sadly, we weren't able to reconcile our differences before he passed away. Now, for the first time since his death, I felt a deep sorrow for him. All his life he had been a tortured, unhappy man unable to fulfill his personal dreams.

Dressed in full Balinese regalia along with the members of Judy and Surya's tour group, we arrived and took seats on folding chairs in the courtyard of the compound facing a *balé* festooned with many offerings and decorations. All the guests received little boxes filled with refreshments—rice cakes, peanuts and containers of water. Everyone was busy socializing while the actual wedding ceremony was taking place privately off to one side in the family temple area. To my amazement, there at the wedding was a guest who looked exactly like a Balinese version of my father!

What is my father doing in Bali?
There aren't any racetracks or card rooms
and the natives are too high-risk to qualify
for health and accident insurance.
But there he is among the wedding guests
on a fold-up rental chair just two rows away
and looking right at me.
Short and stocky, he wears a sarong,
Nehru jacket and funny little wrap-around hat.
Arms crossed, taciturn, as all around him
people are schmoozing and eating.
Is he waiting for me to disappoint him again?

Following the wedding, Judy and I took an excursion to the northeast coastal resort of Amed on the Java Sea within sight of the island of Lombok. One morning, we took a sunrise boat ride with two teenage fishermen from a neighboring fishing village in their *prahu* outrigger…

Across the Lombok Strait,
rising out of the smooth, dark Java sea,
an orange sun frames Mt. Rinjani,
and the sky flashes pink to reveal
scores of amazed eyes
painted on the spear-tipped prows
of the fishing prahus
darting about in search of prey.
Last lit, the toothy smile of our captain,
proud to have his boat filled with plump tourists,
first to head home in the freshening breeze.

From Amed, we spent a few nights at Judy and Surya's. They had offered us their home in lieu of us staying in our *joglo* while they were on tour with their group in North Bali. That way we could experience what living in the compound would be like. We arrived just in time to catch the setting sun backlighting everything in tones of orange and red, as spectacular as the rising sun at Amed. Dining on the verandah, everything was bathed in the pink afterglow. As the full moon rose, we heard a priest chanting across the rice paddies from the nearby town of Mas, along with the liquid, clear tones of a *gamelan* accompanied by a riotous chorus of frogs and crickets.

I sit on the verandah of my Bali home
staring into the black and white batik
of a star-filled sky.

Dag-dug-geledag-geledug…nepak-nepak-nepak

The drums of a neighboring village punctuate
the *kotekan*, interlocking rhythms…

crickets…*nyeet-nyeet*
frogs…*ngerok ngerok*
fireflies…*kunang-kunang*

Jangih goes the night bird
as the *gamelan* bursts…*kebyar!*
Kleneng-kleneng…the bronze pots of the *reong*
ring eddies of sound into the night.

Nang-na-na-ning-na-ning-na-ning-nung-non…
metal-keyed *gangsas* strike fire
off the full moon, then…

Ngenongin-n-n...
the big gong silences all
but the *geradag-geredeg* of my heartbeat
as my spirit ascends.

Waking at dawn, we looked out the bedroom window to
see our home "jo-glowing" as the rising sun struck it...

Thunk-thunk-thunk...
from a distant village
the wooden *kul-kul* bell
signals a new day.

Priests chanting
crickets chirping
farmers planting
bent over my journal
writing.

We met Mari, our furniture guru, for lunch in Ubud at
Cafe Wayan on Monkey Forest Road, then returned to the
joglo. Gesturing dramatically, she stalked the large living room
spouting decorating tips. "One couch go here. Opium table in
front. Rattan chairs on either end of table. No room on *balé* for
second couch. It go by sliding door. There, by breezeway, big
potted plants, one on each side."

Gedé, a shorter and thinner version of his older brother
Surya, watched every move we made around the *joglo* with
his big, warm intelligent eyes so he could do the right job
installing the wiring and fixtures.

Any hopes for moving in before we left were dashed when
Surya fired the architect who couldn't find any skilled workers

to finish the work. Everyone was involved in the construction boom or working for furniture factories. The progress on the house came to a standstill. We had to reconcile ourselves to waiting until our next visit to enjoy our new home...

In Bali, much time is spent waiting...

Drivers with eyes half-lidded
squat at the curb, on the lookout
to snag a tourist or two
quick as lizard tongues spearing flies.
Dragonflies hover over ponds
searching for mosquitoes.
Shopkeepers loll on steps
in hopes passers-by will stop.
Monkeys beg bananas in the forest.
People kneel at temple festivals,
eyes closed, hands open
for the blessed touch of holy water.

***

With only a few weeks before *Nyepi*, the purification ceremonies were now in full swing all over the island. We drove down to Sanur on the southwest coast to view one of the largest of the many processions to the sea. Our driver dropped us off a few blocks from the beach where many Balinese families awaited the approach of the procession from the nearby temple. We seemed to be the only foreigners and hoped to blend right in, dressed for the occasion in our best sarongs and sashes.

Soon we could hear the clanging of the marching *gamelan beleganjur* and watched in awe as at least a hundred women dressed in lacy, tight-fitting *kebayas* and sarongs walked by, carrying elaborate offerings of baskets of fruit, bowls of rice, flowers and incense on their heads. After them came a crowd of people dressed in their temple finery carrying banners, multicolored umbrellas and effigies of the rice goddess, Dewi Sri.

We joined the procession to the beach. There we found a vantage point on a wooden bench among the thousands of celebrants seated on a strip of sand no more than thirty yards wide. A large platform was constructed near the water's edge on which the women placed their offerings. From the bowls full of rice, fruit, flowers and incense, they prepared individual offerings on hand-size, woven leaf pallets which they distributed to the seated celebrants. There was the pleasant buzz of socializing as if there were all the time in the world and absolutely no discomfort at being jammed in together.

Then the priests, dressed in white, sprinkled the assembled with holy water and blessed them. Numerous times, bells were rung and flower petals raised overhead in supplication. A thoughtful gentleman seated in front of us handed us some flowers...

This day before New Year's
we join the procession to the beach
where, minds muddled
with the "busyness" of our lives,
we kneel with hundreds of others
before the altar piled high
with offerings of fruit and flowers.

The old priests chant
sprinkle holy water
ring bells...

Between clasped fingers
we raise flower petals overhead
pray for enlightenment.

In less than an hour, all the festivities had concluded; the platforms taken down, the celebrants departed, and, as if on cue, the tide came in to take away all the offerings strewn about…

Like the tide
prayers flow in and out
with each breath we take…
sweep us clean.

***

On New Year's Eve day, Surya invited us to his family home in Denpasar to work out final arrangements for our partnership and view the New Year's parade extravaganza with the tour group. He met us at the gate to the family compound and welcomed us graciously into the small, low-ceilinged, rectangular living room with its louvered glass windows, a luxury in Bali. This was Surya's old bedroom when he had lived at home.

It reminded us of our first visit thirteen years ago, when our tour group was treated to a marvelous buffet lunch cooked by his sister, Ketut Suryani, and served in this very same room. Inside, on the grass-matted floor, Surya directed us to two cane chairs on either side of a coffee table while he relaxed in a large, easy chair made from big bamboo staves. He proudly handed us an official, notarized bill of sale for our home, and we toasted our new partnership with glasses of Australian wine. Then we got down to business and the plans to complete the house.

Again, Surya apologized for the house not being ready for us. After much searching he had found some new workers but, unfortunately, could not promise when our home would be finished. We reassured him that we had gotten over our disappointment and did not blame him. We set a tentative date for completion of July 1, when daughter Caitlin would be visiting and adding the final touches to the decor.

After our meeting, Judy and I visited with Surya's genial father, Bapak Ketut Gina, and sister Ketut who was baby-sitting his newly arrived nephew, the son of Surya's brother Nyoman, whose family lived in the compound. The old priest lovingly held a puppy as he proudly showed us around. In every available space there were flowers, shrubs and trees. His potted plants hung on the special *balé* for sleeping, receiving guests and family activities, next to the entrance to the compound. The family temple area with its many shrines, where Ketut had been married just a few weeks before, lay in the most auspicious, northeast or *kaja-kangin* corner, beautifully landscaped like a small park. Next to the kitchen in the least auspicious south or *kelod* direction was the old priest's pride and joy, a little Garden of Eden with banana, jackfruit, papaya and mango trees, ferns, hibiscus, frangipani, birds of paradise and other flowers and even a small vegetable plot.

Little did we know this would be the last time we would see him. This sweet, gentle, loving and wise father, husband, priest and respected village elder would pass away the following month, shortly after our return to the States. Well beloved for his service to his people, Bapak Gina had held the position of anti-drug enforcement officer; and from his young manhood on, and even after his retirement, he continued working for the office of religion on Balinese customary law or *adat...*

We learned much from Bapak Gina,
who had kept his family together
in this simple compound
where he cultivated the earth
as did his ancestors for 400 years.
Survivor and hero of the Dutch and Japanese
occupation and the Indonesian Civil War,
he carries his puppy tenderly in his arms
while he shows us his flourishing garden
well-tended grounds and the shrine
behind which some of his ashes
will soon be buried in a coconut shell.

When the tour group arrived, we headed off through Surya's neighborhood past the local temple. His neighbors hailed him as they mounted their *ogoh-ogoh* on a bamboo pallet that would be carried on the shoulders of the young men of Surya's *banjar* in the big parade through Denpasar. The giant monster was a modern incarnation of the evil witch Rangda in high fashion dress with an expression that showed she vainly considered herself quite beautiful.

After a short walk, we arrived at the first hotel in Bali, the plain, squat, stucco colonial style Bali Beach, built by the Dutch. There we had an Indonesian rice table dinner served buffet style while a Balinese Johnny Mathis crooned kitschy love songs. Outside on the large verandah adjacent to the main thoroughfare, chairs were set up for the spectators. We had front row seats to view the parade.

Banjar youth groups from all over Bali vied with each other for the prizes awarded to the best, most fanciful creations. Before our stunned eyes, the giant monsters were borne on wooden pallets, jeeps, trucks and pulled on wagons by hordes of Balinese teenagers, running and yelling at the top of their lungs over the clanging, marching *gamelans*. I never saw anyone sweat like the young man who ran at top speed as he thrust a flaming torch into a barrel of gasoline with one hand and swigged water from a bottle with his other!

Close to a hundred *ogoh-ogoh* careened down the street. Giant effigies of lurching Rangdas, tongues lolling, claws outstretched, threatened to grab innocent bystanders. A slimy skinned alien was being born out of a demon as she was being impregnated by her grotesque lover. There was a Rangda dressed in a British Union Jack and one on a surfboard. Any evil spirits about would have fled in panic at the sight of such monstrosities…

> Tonight, New Year's eve,
> the dreaded *ogoh-ogoh*
> with their lolling tongues,
> bug-eyes and outstretched claws
> scare off the evil spirits
> who hold captive our true selves.

Four hours later, exhausted and exhilarated, we tumbled into the waiting vans. At midnight, lights had gone out over the entire island as did all electricity for the 24 hours of *Nyepi*. Surya handed out packaged lunches for the holiday since cooking was forbidden and the Balinese fast. We planned to join them. The three-quarter moon barely lit the way through the empty streets of Denpasar and into the countryside. Only careless foreigners were abroad on this haunted night.

Around every curve, I expected to encounter an evil spirit reveling in its last night of freedom. The driver dropped us off, grinding gears as he roared away. We hurried down the moonlit path into the rice fields back to our room at Oka

Wati's to fall into the deep, dreamless sleep of the dead, ready to be reborn on *Nyepi* morning.

*****

At dawn we awoke to a magnificent silence. Gone were the rude sounds of motors. Even the garrulous roosters seemed to be obeying the law that nothing must be louder than the sounds of nature. Although the sky was still dark, there was an unusual lightness in the atmosphere...

New Year's morning...
All over the island
motors are silent
people stay home
fast, meditate,
speak only to wish each other well.

On the verandah, writing in our journals, our houseman, Nyoman, wished us a happy *Nyepi,* offering us sweet rice cakes wrapped in banana leaves, a special holiday treat with fruit and coffee and then, after a quick apology, left...

As we sip strong coffee
and breathe in the silence,
our houseman announces
that on this day of purification,
he must quickly return to his family
and so will be unable to clean our room.

Looking up up from my journal, I saw a white dove...

On Nyepi morning,
the dove carefully steps around

the warrior statue and
does not peck the rice grains
on the offering plate.

She waddles up the steps
and hops onto our table
to feast on the remains of our meal
as we begin our fast.

Like a film in slow motion, the delicious morning passed as the sun rose to reveal more and more of the lush scene around us. By the front steps were two small stone statues of plump little guardians carrying clubs to ward off the evil doers. Beyond was a well tended garden bordered by orchids, birds of paradise, bougainvillea, gardenia, hibiscus, sweet smelling frangipani and a meandering path. Banana and coconut palms along with graceful Norfolk pines spread their leaves to shield us from the bright sunlight breaking through the morning mist. Adjacent to our room, the steep jungle ravine that had lain hidden in shadow, festooned with vines and creepers, came into view.

Each petal, leaf and blade of grass appeared framed in its own light. How many times before had I looked and not really seen the total uniqueness and beauty of each living thing?

The sun inches higher
clouds dissolve to reveal
purple volcanoes.
Cicadas buzz longer, louder.
Each frond, petal, blade of grass
stands out as our minds clear.

Keeping to tradition, we spent the day in meditation, reading and writing. That night, the electricity remained off...

After twelve hours of day,
on the first night of the New Year
the whole island is dark
so we can see how to put
our lives back in balance.

The next morning, refreshed and renewed, we said our farewells to Oka Wati and staff.

The flight home passed quickly. I was thankful for the time to record my last impressions of the trip. More than ever, Judy and I were ready for a future that would include our beautiful new Bali home.

***

Back home in California, I heard an author being interviewed on NPR say he never wrote anything that wasn't transformative for him; I realized that was also true for me. By the end of May 2000, I had completed outlining my Bali travel journals and began work on the first draft of the manuscript.

Little did I know I had been preparing for a difficult time. Once my father passed away, my ninety-year-old mother's creeping dementia accelerated, and soon she had to make the difficult move from Southern California to a care home near us in Santa Cruz where, as her primary guardian, I took charge of her welfare. If I could make things easier and give her some joy in her last years, I would be content. But the transition would be difficult in this new and strange environment.

In July, Caitlin traveled to Bali where she worked with

Surya and his crew to bring the remodel to completion. She outfitted the kitchen, hung Balinese paintings and added many personal touches. How exciting it was to get her emails that kept us updated on her progress! In August, Caitlin's beautiful photos of our *joglo* popped up on the computer screen in time for Judy's and my 38th anniversary. I was so glad I had re-established my bond with her in Bali.

Shortly after we returned from Bali that spring, Surya's father and the father of Pak Sumandhi, one of the *gamelan* gurus who came to teach at UCSC, also named Gina, died within a few weeks of each other. Sumandhi's father had been the *dalang* or master shadow puppeteer of his village of Tunjuk for many years. Both were highly respected and beloved, fierce defenders of Balinese tradition and freedom who had participated in the birth and childhood of their new nation. Each patriarch had died fulfilled, bringing together his karma with his dharma, his responsibility for his own actions with his service to others, his life with his work.

The lives of both men testified to the fact that spiritual transformation isn't an instant miracle; it is a slow, lifelong process...

> *Like a gamelan that can*
> *ring an infinity of melodies*
> *with just four metal keys,*
> *we play the changes*
> *in our full lives*
> *with the few notes we know.*

V
THE DREAM COME TRUE
Fifth Trip—April 16 through May 12, 2001

Judy and I talked and dreamed of being in our beautiful home in Bali, but was it possible? We made some tentative plans. My mother's dementia was steadily advancing. She would forget from day to day if I had come to visit and complain that I never came.

In early April she suffered two falls that landed her in the hospital. After the second fall, she had to be moved to a full care facility, and I considered canceling the trip. To supplement the nursing and care staff, we hired two young women for a few hours daily to keep her company. They made a big difference. Assuring us we had done all we could, everyone urged us to go on with our Bali plans. My brother and our daughters promised to visit and keep a close eye on her while we were away.

My worry over my mother brought up the old fear for my own survival from the well of insecurity inside me since childhood. Growing up, I never knew when my father would gamble away our savings, quit or lose his job, forcing us to move.

One night just before we left for Bali, I rented a movie that had a powerful effect on me...

I tell myself it's just a Hollywood movie...
The young boy running away from home

becomes an accidental victim
of his terrorist father's explosives.
Stumbling down the middle of the street,
he grips his belly to keep his guts from spilling.
Jeff Bridges plays a watchful neighbor,
who saves him from being hit by a car
and rushes him to the hospital...

Where's the hero to rescue me?
After a week on the road of no sales,
unable to recoup his losses at the poker table,
my father throws down his cards,
comes home and pours out his anger
at the dinner table where my mother
waits, crying for her lost husband
and a son who has been saying goodbye for years.

Besides worries for my mother, my thoughts of sunny Bali were clouded over by new responsibilities. We were no longer tourist birds who rented a temporary perch in paradise but absentee homeowners, 6,000 miles across an ocean. Also, what would it be like to be three miles away from the conveniences in Ubud or a hundred meters into the rice paddies from the main road with no car and no phone? Or much worse, were we New Age colonialists, exploiting the natives?

***

As soon as we arrived, we became aware of the changes Bali had gone through in the past year. Everywhere we looked, new construction was going on, anticipating an increased number of tourists now that Megawati had won the election and promised to stabilize the government. But tourism remained half of what it was before the fall of Suharto and the ensuing governmental chaos. Bids for independence by the individual states of Timor, Irian Jaya and Madura, internecine wars between Muslims and Christians, and runaway inflation all played their part. Now more and more homestays, resorts, hotels, restaurants and galleries stood empty as tourists were warned away from Indonesia by the U.S. State Department, and travelers from all over the globe headed elsewhere.

We parked on the road next to the Genta Gallery. Hyperventilating with excitement, we passed the welcoming Ganesha statue at the head of the path to our *joglo*. Sure enough, there was the old mother sow lying in the mud alongside an unsightly pile of garbage, fatter than ever. After we passed the modern concrete and glass gallery, we were once again in old, rural Bali with the rice fields on one side of the path and pasture on the other, where a sweet faced mother cow and her two calves grazed on the long grass. Just past their bamboo pen was the large, carved wooden gate in our compound wall open to receive us!

More beautiful than we remembered, the garden next to the pond was flourishing with flowering shrubs, the moat surrounding the *joglo* full and covered with water lilies and flowering lotus...

Crossing an ocean to Bali.
like flies landing on lily pads
in the garden pond,
we are home.

Surya's brother-in-law, Agus, caretaker of the compound, greeted us, taking great pleasure explaining everything in English. When we complimented him, his serious, anxious-to-please expression broke into a big, toothy smile as he smoothed back his long hair tied in a ponytail.

Sure enough, there was all the beautiful teak, mahogany and rattan furniture filling the living area, almost thirty foot square. Across the breezeway in the stone building, the kitchen, spacious and serviceable with built-in cabinets and sink, refrigerator and propane-run stovetop and small dining table, was completed. In the bedroom sat the king-size, dark mahogany, four-poster canopy bed covered by mosquito netting at one end and the large armoire at the other. The bedroom window was enlarged, giving a view of the adjacent open field filled with palms and tall grass. Off the bedroom, through French doors and down a small flight of stairs, was the completed bathroom partially open to the blue Bali sky, enclosed by a semi-circular, ochre colored wall.

While we were "ooohing and ahhing," Nyoman Tomblos, the gardener, greeted us in his quiet, unassuming manner. He had followed Surya and Judy from their old place in Kedewaton and now worked here. Every day he brought fresh offerings and placed them all around the compound. His slight figure soon became a familiar sight, carrying in one graceful, upturned hand the tray filled with daily offerings on tiny banana leaf pallets, incense sticks smoking.

Agus asked if there was anything he might do to improve the *joglo*? We were so overcome, we couldn't think of a thing. But after a few days, we had a small list with minor items such as lowering the outlets so we could plug in our table lamps, lacquering the bamboo platform that served as a bridge over the moat in the front, and putting in window screens in key places to keep out the mosquitoes. Agus quickly responded, "I do, I do!" And he did, quickly, neatly and inventively.

We were ecstatic guests in our own home. Before

unpacking, I began taking photos from every conceivable angle inside and outside the *joglo* while Judy rearranged the furniture. We were "running on empty" after our long trip but were so excited we couldn't stop. I took great pleasure in putting all my writing materials in the three drawers of the mahogany desk and lining up my books, including the journal, along the top of the desk.

In the fridge was a welcome dinner, prepared by Wayan and Kadek, the young housekeepers who tended our two homes. And what a meal—two kinds of chicken, roasted and sautéed, a vegetable dish of tempeh, spinach and bean sprouts with an excellent *gado-gado* sauce, rice and deviled eggs.

While we ate, we watched the red sunset afterglow and heard the first sounds of evening. The frogs started up in the moat along with the crickets. Soon the sliver of a moon rose and tipped its way through the light clouds. The breeze died down, leaving the air perfectly still in the translucent atmosphere of the tropical night.

From across the ravine in the direction of the village of Mas, the resonant, deep-throated voice of a priest chanting in the classic, ancient Kawi language lulled us to sleep.

I awoke abruptly in the first gray light of dawn to a second visitation from my father and hurried out to the terrace to sit on the top step of the stairs leading down to the garden with my journal.

Watching the dawn sky change from red-streaked gray to purple and gold, I tried to recall my father's expression in the dream—not that of the new loving father doting on his baby, nor the old, embittered man he became...

The frogs have fallen silent.
A priest's plaintive chant

echoes across the rice fields.
Through the mosquito netting,
a sliver of moon disappears behind a cloud.

I awake to see my dead father
standing at the foot of my bed.

"Why have you come, Dad?"

He does not answer.

"I have carried out your dying wish
to take care of Mom...
Is there something more I should do?"

He is gone.

The vision became clearer. No longer did he hold his anger tightly in his jaw. His thick eyebrows slack over his soft brown eyes, he looked sad and tired...

6 a.m. I squat on the terrace steps, writing.
On the fountain in the pond, the stone frog
has climbed its mate's back for a better look
at the vermilion and gold-streaked sky.
A dove pads down the path
then stops, cranes its neck at me.

Suddenly, I knew why he had come...

Father, it is not too late.
I shall spread your ashes

here on this rich, tropical earth
to nourish our forgiveness.

If I forgave my father, perhaps I could forgive myself and realize my full potential as an artist and a human being. This would truly be "living the dream" of being a loving and creative person...and my father could rest in peace.

***

Just before eight, a motorbike pulled in and parked just inside the gate. Dressed in uniform white blouses and blue skirts, two teenage girls doffed their helmets and headed over to introduce themselves. Plump and boisterous, Kadek was in the lead. Behind her came the thin, shy Wayan who walked with a slight limp. She let the outgoing Kadek do all the talking. We thanked them for keeping up the place so well and gave them envelopes containing their salaries. Kadek explained they worked every morning until noon. Afternoons, they attended the nearby tourist school to study English and learn how to serve foreigners. "We will make you very happy," she assured us, as Wayan nodded quietly, a smile flickering across her face.

That first day, our driver, Pak Dewa, took us to the village of Sukawati and the studio of a stone sculptor friend of his, Pak Mudiana. There we chose three musicians for the little pedestals that stood in the moat on the east side of the house and a statue with frogs for the pond in front. The jovial Mudiana threw in a few more little frogs for good measure.

I coaxed Nyoman, the gardener, whom we knew was a fine musician, to play the bamboo *tingklik*. I had a bamboo flute or *suling* with a scale that came close to matching the notes of the *tingklik*. Sitting across from each other...

Playing together,
Nyoman and I,
flute solos over
tingklik ostinato,
our souls in harmony.

The following day, the handsomely dressed Pak Mudiana stopped by on his way to his temple's birthday festival to deliver the statues. He carefully placed the musicians, each on its own pedestal, giving them their first "holy water" dousing...

Three dreamy-looking, potbellied, stone musicians,
a flute player, a drummer and a time keeper
about to strike his brass pot, have arrived
to cool their feet in the pond by our home.
They accompany the insect dancers
who swim around them during the day.
In the evening, they rest and let the frog gamelan play.

Three days later, our first guests, one of my oldest childhood friends, Gordon Brisker and his wife Cindy, arrived from Australia, where Gordon was teaching jazz at the University of Sydney.

Once again, Bali worked its magic, bringing back childhood memories. Both Gordon and I had mothers who instilled in us a love of music. Every Saturday morning, they would take us by the hands up the long hill through the iron gate in the stone wall to the old mansion, the Cincinnati Conservatory of Music, where I imagined the muses lived. There, in a rhythm band, we banged drums, tinkled triangles, shook rattles. When we got older, we took violin and clarinet lessons from master musicians who played with the Cincinnati symphony and opera...

On Saturday mornings, I fled with
my beautiful, green-eyed mother muse,
from the cramped apartment
in the sooty, yellow brick building
and my father's anger...
took the clangy streetcar
that clicked on the rails, intricate rhythms
I beat out on the back of the wooden seat.

Crunching the fallen leaves,
hand-in-hand we hurried up the steep hill,
the long driveway overhung with dark oaks,
to the Cincinnati Conservatory of Music.

I push open the heavy door and music
from everywhere flows over me.
Leaving her downstairs in the parlor,
I climb the creaky stairs
my violin case jiggling in my sweaty hand.
Glimpsing my reflection in the shiny banister,
heady with the scent of the deep, rich, black walnut,
I pause to catch my breath at the third floor landing
before I head down the dark hall
to the room where my teacher waits.

Gordon and I played in high school band and performed in jazz combos at social functions for pocket money. From high school, Gordon attended the famed Berklee School of Music in Boston and went on to become an acclaimed professional jazz instrumentalist and composer-arranger while I went on to get a master's degree in creative writing to teach college English composition and literature. I always wondered what would have happened if I had continued to follow my first love, music, to Boston with Gordon?

In the late afternoon, we drove to the village of Petulu, a natural government preserve maintained by the villagers. About an hour before sunset, hundreds of herons circled in from all over Bali to roost in the large, spreading trees. Within minutes the trees seemed to be covered with snow. We sat on a rickety picnic bench at the official tourist observation station, a shack with a long, thatch-covered verandah, sipping Cokes and looking through antique binoculars across the dirt road that traversed the small village up into the trees.

Curiously, the herons started to gather here in '65 just after the bloody revolution that led to the fall of the WWII liberator and founder of the Republic of Indonesia, Sukarno. The villagers believe the birds are possessed by the souls of the dead victims of that tragic civil war...

No matter how we meet our end,
at sunset our souls will continue to gather
along with the herons in Petulu.

In Munduk, I took Gordon to meet Pak Terip. From the main road along the ridge top, we climbed slowly down the steep hillside to his home. Pak Terip's *gamelan kebyar* had taken second place in Bali at the Art Festival the previous summer—a very rare occurrence indeed for such a small village to outshine *gamelans* from all over Bali. And now the Gong Munduk was in great demand. As we sipped coffee served by his smiling wife in fragile china cups, he showed us his album with pictures of their recent tour to France.

Some of the players had never been out of Munduk and none had ever left Bali before this tour. Later, we heard from Surya that in the heart of Paris, the gourmet capital of the Western world, the simple, poor villagers were too intimidated to leave their hotel rooms, where they subsisted on packages of Top Ramen!

Barely communicating in hodgepodge English, I asked Terip if he had any flutes for sale, and he brought out two he had recently made. I played them and asked Gordon to help me decide on one. But he just smiled and shook his head, claiming Balinese music was completely new to him, so he couldn't be any judge.

Later that day we swapped stories of our early married lives, together with our wives at dinner in the elevated pergola at Puri Lumbung overlooking the volcanoes to the south and east that rose into the enormous starlit night sky. Gordon talked about studying Buddhism and practicing nonattachment which he found extremely difficult. We agreed it only happens moment by moment, if at all. I shared that, in Bali, I had always been unable to hold onto any anger or negative feelings very long. Here, everything is in a constant state of change—the unpredictable weather, the intuitive people, the teeming nature, and the bad memories of the past lose their power over me.

Even though I was tired from the day's hike through the rain forest around the volcanic lakes of Bratan and Tamblingan and was pleasantly cool in our rice barn room, I spent a fitful night dealing with the regret of not following my old friend into music, but then, in the morning...

After a night of confused dreams of loss,
dawn comes and my vision clears
to reveal mountain ridge upon ridge,
the Java Sea and beyond...
my life on its own path

***

After Gordon and Cindy left Bali, I returned to our routine of waking at dawn to write...

Seated in the rattan easy chair with my feet up on the hassock on the shady south side of the *joglo*, I write in my journal. Judy does the same. The morning light is lemony and diffused, the air fresh, with a slightly chill edge from the night before.

When my concentration flags, I have only to look out the sliding door to the garden and the pond to become reinspired. Life is all around us at every moment. Cicadas buzzing, birds singing, frogs croaking, the sound of a distant motorbike coughing, priests chanting. Anything and everything seems possible!

I wished Mom could experience some peace at the end of her days. Here the elderly are respected and useful, helping take care of the children and the family compound. When finally they pass on, they will be cremated, their souls joyfully released from their suffering bodies.

I was getting so laid back I continually confused *besok*, "tomorrow" with *kemarin*, "yesterday," telling people I would see them "yesterday" or I saw something "tomorrow"...

If I use the Balinese word for "tomorrow"
for "yesterday" and the word for "yesterday"
for "tomorrow," all days in Bali become "today."

Ironically, I had a lot in common with my poor mom. Time had collapsed for her just as it had for me. Maybe when I returned to Santa Cruz, it would seem to her as if I had just seen her *kemarin*. Telling myself I needn't feel guilty for not being with her, I was thankful to have the peace of mind to begin preparing myself here in Bali for her approaching death and to enjoy the precious time I had left on earth.

On our last day in Bali we planned a goodbye luncheon, prepared by Wayan and Kadek, for the whole staff including Dewa, our driver, and us. Artistically arranged buffet style were festive dishes including fried chicken, tempeh, *gado-gado*, greens, spiced eggs, rice, and sliced, assorted fruit for dessert. Everyone waited for Judy and I to serve ourselves, but we insisted that the Western style was to serve the guests first. Everyone filled their plates and then took seats on the edge of the *balé* or on the floor to eat. After eating for a while in silence, as was the Balinese custom, all formality was dropped and the teasing and joking began.

Agus poked gentle fun at Nyoman Tomblos, the slender, shy bachelor, declaring it was time he got married and Kadek, the plump, ebullient housegirl, was a likely candidate. Kadek took it in good spirits, laughing along with the rest of us. Even Nyoman couldn't help smiling. After we finished eating, I made a little speech telling them how much I appreciated them all and was afraid I would wake after my first night back in California and think the whole Bali trip had been a dream!

Agus insisted I have some of the vodka he had brought just for the occasion. We made a number of toasts, and I kicked up my heels and went into a Russian *kazatsky*. Everyone laughed, even shy Tomblos...

We sit down together to feast
and celebrate the world at peace.

Our last day arrived soon enough...

It is the day we leave Bali.
I stop packing to sit and stare
at my reflection in the pond
and let the goldfish nibble on my toes.
Wherever I go, I am home.

***

I was glad for the time on the return flight to take spiritual stock of what I had gained over the past fifteen years of our Balinese odyssey. Judy and I had immersed ourselves in the Balinese culture, the music and the fine art, had a working understanding and a deep respect for the customs and religion. In Bali, where evil is not denied but included as part of the cosmic scheme, I had begun to exorcise my personal demons, reconcile with my father who had died before we could resolve our disagreements, and even forgive him.

Within a few weeks of our return, my dear mother passed away. I realized all the many gifts she had given me. Her last was keeping her tenuous grip on life until I returned. After her death, I wrote about my last evening with her...

I sit at her bedside
hoping she will recognize me,
tell me something I need to know,
but a stroke has left her mute.

What do her glazed eyes see?
Through her frail hand, I feel
the bond between us unbroken.

"I love you, Mom...Can you hear me?"

Her bird-thin chest shudders and is still.
Then she gasps, jerking her hand out of my grasp
and claws at the sheet that barely covers her.

"It's OK, Mom...you can go," I whisper,
wiping the saliva from her mouth.
"Everything's all right, Mom."

I take her hand once again
and feel no answering pressure.
Still I can hear her jagged breath,
watch her ribs convulse.

"Remember all the good times
we had together?"

She turns her head away from me.
Her withered hand slips out of mine,
fingers still, eyes closed.
At last she breathes easy in sleep.

"Everything's all right, Mom."

I rise from her bedside to leave her
for the last time.

VI
AT HOME IN BALI
Sixth Trip—June 26 through July 28, 2002

After raving to our friends and relatives, we simply had to return; so we began planning for the following summer. The year whirled by and before we knew it, we were crossing the little bamboo bridge into our new home, which had undergone a complete transformation!

Surya's brother, Nyoman, had taken the place of Nyoman Tomblos who quit to pursue his artistic career full time. He was doing an excellent job as the new gardener. The linear borders separating the houses from each other and from the grounds were full of new plantings.

Next to the rice barn, in the northwest corner closest to the holy Mt. Agung and taking the place of the older stone shrine, was the crowning glory of the compound, ornately carved from white stone, the three meter-high *padmasana* with a seat at the top. Agus and Nyoman had built a wall around it and planted the enclosure to make a real temple…

Home now, we invite the gods to visit…
sit on the white stone padmasana
and watch over us.

The area below the curving stone steps that led to the lower terrace of our property was thoroughly cleared of the long, pesky *alang-alang* grass. The terraces extending out from the steps were full of young plantings, and a small clump of thick yellow bamboo grew next to the stone wall that bordered the back of the compound. All the repairs and improvements on the house had been made, including mosquito proofing and increasing the ventilation in the bedroom with sliding screens in front of the picture window that looked out to the open fields, and now a window in the kitchen brought in more light.

Since Judy and Surya weren't due to arrive until the first week in July, we rented their house for our first visitors, my brother Ray and his wife, Chris. This would be our first time together since Mom's funeral the previous year.

The next morning, while Ray and Chris slept in, Judy and I rose at dawn to write. As we had breakfast overlooking the garden, we watched Wayan pick red hibiscus blossoms...

It is Balinese winter and
the height of the dry season.
The garden must be constantly watered
daily offerings made,
relationships tended with loving care.

As children, Ray and I were brought together not only by our love but by being victims of domestic wars in our insecure household. As adults, we had reacted by making totally separate lives in different places, rarely seeing each other. Ray was a successful and innovative business man; I chose an alternative lifestyle in teaching and the arts that brought little monetary success but much satisfaction.

All our lives, our bitter, insecure parents loved us but could not stop playing us, one against the other, complaining to me that Ray was selfish and uncaring, insulated by his money and to him that I was a "beatnik" who would never amount to anything. We let them come between us and went for long periods not speaking to each other. In recent years, we took a united stand not to allow them to complain behind our backs. And since my father had died five years previously, we began to build a deeper relationship.

A large dragonfly buzzed in from the garden...

Instead of my brother who lies asleep,
a dragonfly is our first morning guest,
in one door and out the other.

Having flown such a long way,
may my brother stay long enough
for us to become close again.

Later, while Ray was getting a post-jet lag massage, Dewa and I sipped beers in a nearby restaurant overlooking the rice paddies. I noticed the rice farmers were all older men, their sinewy arms and legs taut as ropes as they bent over working. One was using a long pole to level out the muddy field while, following him, his partner painstakingly transplanted the young rice shoots from a wooden tray.

I asked Dewa why I didn't see any younger men laboring in the fields, and he explained that the young men did not want to work as hard as their fathers. I asked what would happen after this older generation died off. He replied that already Bali could barely grow and harvest enough rice to feed itself, and the situation was getting worse.

Every once in a while the rice farmers looked up from their work to glance in our direction. "Do they envy us, relaxing and enjoying ourselves?" I queried. "Not really," Dewa replied. "It is their karma. They enjoy their work even though it is so hard." What a different view of life!

> *Even if the gods were not watching,*
> *the Balinese would still make offerings*
> *plant green seedlings in thick mud*
> *lay red hibiscus flowers in a clean sink*
> *make yellow rice on holidays*
> *and, like good tourists,*
> *we would spend all our rupiah.*

Were the young Balinese men unduly influenced by us? Here they were training for the tourist and computer industry when neither could employ the majority of them. In Surya's family, Agus and Nyoman trained to be veterinarians and Gedé, an engineer. All three do not work in their professions.

Would Bali soon join the rest of the world with a consumer-based rather than a producer-based economy? In the Ubud supermarket, there were more imported items than Indonesian. When I tried to find an Indonesian brand of peanut butter, or better yet, raw peanuts and a grinder to make our own *gado-gado,* all we found was Skippy!

Less and less land in Bali is available for cultivation. Sixteen years ago, Monkey Forest Road was a country road with a few stores, where you could still could glimpse farmers working in the fields or herding their ducks. Now it was chock-a-block with stores and resorts from one end to the other, including an Italian import store in the first two-story building in Ubud.

***

Chris came down with a slight case of Bali belly. Judy stayed with her in the compound while Ray and I journeyed to the holy mother temple of Bali, Besakih on Mt. Agung. The place was jammed with tourists. Despite our objections, hiring a guide was mandatory. As we climbed the steep path to the temple, past stalls where everything from Mickey Mouse tee shirts to bananas was sold, we were slow moving targets for the aggressive hawkers. The sun was out, the skies perfectly clear so that the imposing temples with their multiple, black thatched, pagoda-roofed *merus* stood out in sharp relief against the azure sky...

After years apart, my brother and I
come together in Bali.
As we hike up the steep slope of
Genung Agung, the holy mountain,
careful not to trip on our long sarongs
and our differences, Ray confesses
his jealousy of my childhood
closeness with our dead father.

I tell him how Dad and I
would play catch until
I would throw the ball wild.
Then he'd hurl down the glove
and walk off without a word.

We trudge up the mountain,
retreating into ourselves.
Hot, tired and about to turn back,
our guide urges us just a little farther
for the view from the temple
of Dewa Iswara, God of Enlightenment.

Mounting a long flight of stairs,
we stand, breathless, on the parapet
looking down on the many shrines
with their tiered pagoda roofs
reaching towards heaven.
Below, all of South Bali rolls towards the sea.

I break the silence to remind Ray
his name means "light of the world."
Shielding my eyes, I see him
framed against the brilliant sun, smiling.

On our way back to Lod Tunduh, we made a stop at the *gamelan* factory of Pak Gableran. There, the ornately carved, painted and gilded wooden cases that hold the metal keys are made and the keys themselves forged, as are the bronze pots and small gongs, all by hand, with pit fires and implements that date back to the Bronze Age—hammers, tongs, bellows, etc. No one was working at the time, but each step in the process could be seen quite clearly. There were row upon row of unfinished cases, piles of recently forged keys and sets of finished instruments that still gave off the heady aroma of wood, fresh paint and turpentine.

At Pak Gableran's I picked up two flutes with the same tuning as the one I used in the *gamelan* in Santa Cruz. While I tested the flutes, Ray went around the large showroom crammed with instruments, banging on gongs, bronze pots and the keys of the *gangsa* metallophones just like a little kid in a toy store. This was the playful younger brother I had always loved.

***

Ray and Chris left for a week in Munduk and a beach resort in Pemuteran on the northwest coast, leaving me free to accept the invitation of my friend and guru, Pak Nyoman Wenten to join him at the Flower Mountain World Music Center, perched on the spectacular Ayung River gorge outside the village of Payangan, a twenty-minute drive from downtown Ubud. Wenten directed the Balinese *gamelans* at Cal Arts and UCLA and had come to Santa Cruz to conduct workshops for our gamelan. He had co-founded the Center in the '70s. He taught there every summer on his yearly pilgrimage back to Bali, where he maintained his family home in the village of Sading.

This summer was special, marking the first Payangan World Music Festival. It would be unique, presenting classic *gamelan* with many kinds of ethnic and new music. Pak Wenten asked me to perform as a guest soloist on clarinet with the student *gamelan* on a fusion piece he had composed called *"Titi Alit"* or "Little Bridges."

Arriving early, Judy and I relaxed as we waited for Wenten...

On a hot afternoon in Bali,
I recline on the cool tile,
take refuge from the heat
in the shade of an open pavilion
where, seated cross-legged,
musicians raise curved wooden hammers,
bend like bamboo stalks in the breeze
to strike the seven iron keys
of the Gamelan Selonding of Tengganan
as I, slowly and steadily, play out
the melody and countermelody of my life.

Soon back from his errands in town, the plump, jovial Bob Brown, the director of the Center and a professor of ethnic musicology at the University of California, San Diego, offered to take us on a tour. He built the Center on land he had purchased in a natural bowl, nestled into the side of the steep river gorge. We descended the stone steps of the path, winding through the luxuriant growth past the pavilions where the classes were held.

On the lowest one, another old friend and guru, Pak Sumandhi, was rehearsing with the student *gamelan* a most beautiful traditional piece called *"Hujan Mas"* or "Golden Rain" to be performed at the Payangan Festival.

We were watching, entranced, legs dangling off the edge of the *balé* when Wenten arrived. Spying us, his handsome face lit up, and we embraced. Apologizing to Pak Sumandhi for his lateness, he immediately sat down, picked up the Balinese two-headed drum and began playing. With a quick smile and a nod, he directed me to accompany him on *ceng-ceng*, the small crash cymbals, which I had never played before. They keep a regular pattern to complement the drum, louder or softer depending on the music. In typical Balinese fashion, no directions were given. After I tried once, Wenten took the little cymbals out of my hands to show me how they should be played.

Pak Sumandhi's rehearsal over, I got out my clarinet and joined the *gamelan* to play Wenten's captivating composition...

> *Nurturing each other's art*
> *in Bali's rich soil*
> *true friendship blooms.*

A few days later, Nyoman Sedana invited us to attend his *banjar's* temple *odalan* birthday celebration. He would be the *dalang* or puppet master for a performance of Wayang Wong, puppet play without a screen to be performed in the day time in contrast to the Wayang Kulit shadow puppet play, performed at night. He was particularly desirous of having Wenten attend one of his first performances since becoming a full-fledged Ph.D. at the University of Georgia. I made arrangements for us all, along with Wenten's and Nanik's students from Cal Arts, to take a trip out to Sedana's Banjar Gubat.

We parked in the countryside and walked down the road lit only by the full moon. The performance took place alongside the small *banjar* temple right in the road.

As I had expected, it was love at first sight for my two guru-friends. After the performance, they posed for pictures and Sedana proudly handed Wenten a copy of his thesis.

Now every day was full of music and adventure...

We wake to the tune of motors,
insects, birds and a gamelan orchestra.
Our thoughts shimmer
with every shade of green
as the leaves sway
in the early morning breeze.
Here and there, red and yellow hibiscus.
What joys, what surprises will the day bring?

The following Saturday, we met Sedana at the Bali Arts Festival at the Art Center in Denpasar. No longer the young graduate student of 1997 in formal *baju* and sarong, wearing an official host's badge and anxious to impress, now he was a professor, dressed casually in jeans and sport shirt.

As we enjoyed a late lunch at a *warung* on the Art Center grounds, I got a call on the cell phone from Pak Wenten who invited Judy and I to attend his nephew's wedding reception that evening in Sading. Not having time to go home and change, Pak Wenten insisted we come directly. He assured us that he could provide us with traditional Balinese costumes.

When we arrived at Wenten's compound expecting to find a hubbub of activity, we found it practically deserted. He welcomed us and announced we were operating on typically Balinese *jam karet*, "rubber time." "No hurry, no worry," he joked as he showed us to the guest bedroom where complete Balinese outfits where laid out, including a *kebaya* for Judy with a sarong, sash, and belt, and a sarong with a *kain* wrapper to be worn over it, ornately embroidered with gold thread and a headband for me. Then he handed us towels so we could take showers. We even had time for a nap.

The wedding was taking place at the next village south in Wenten's relatives' compound. The courtyard was festooned with hanging *cili* coconut leaf decorations, cut, woven and plaited into filigreed, hourglass-shaped figures. Off to one side, a *balé* was overflowing with offerings. The typical folding chairs were set up in rows between the sleeping pavilions and the family shrines. Next to the kitchen on the opposite side of the courtyard, the buffet tables were set up. Going through the reception line, Wenten graciously introduced us as his good friends and special guests to the bride and his nephew, the groom, and his family.

Nuts and sweets were served while an abundance of sumptuous dishes were being laid out on the buffet tables— various curries and stews of lamb, pork, chicken and fish, skewers of chicken and pork *saté* and chopped vegetable *lawar*. As soon as everything had placed, without an announcement the guests began lining up and filling their plates. Meanwhile, we were entertained by a *rindik* ensemble made up of two bamboo *tingklik*, a flute, loud *ceng-ceng* hand cymbals and a gong.

Wenten ate hurriedly and then bounded up with two cameras around his neck to take video and still pictures of everyone. While people were eating and socializing, the bride and groom circulated, greeting everyone individually. The groom was dressed like a king in his embroidered tunic, gold leaf sarong and headband with a sword slung around one shoulder and across his back. The bride was equally regal in her richly patterned *kebaya*, sarong and stunning golden headdress. Returning to our table, Wenten brought over the handsome couple to meet us and pose for a photo together. Then he asked me to use his still camera to take a snapshot of them with Nanik and him...

We take photos of the Balinese,
and they take photos of us,
while the gods look on, amused.

After introducing us to his large family, the irrepressible Wenten joined the musical ensemble on the second bamboo *tingklik*. When it was time to leave, Wenten and the effusive father of the groom accompanied us out to the crowded road to bid us a warm goodbye.

***

Ray and Chris returned from their seashore and mountain trip to Pemuteran and Munduk absolutely ecstatic. Saying our goodbyes, I told them how much I appreciated their help and support for Mom after Dad had passed away, and they thanked me for my care during Mom's last few years in Santa Cruz. Then Ray took me aside to confide that he never felt closer to me. I told him I felt the same...

After many years, we come together in Bali...
the breach healed, the bond resealed.
For loving brothers, there's time to begin anew.

***

The two weeks of rehearsals passed quickly and soon came the day for the first Payangan festival. This was another dream come true—a world music festival in a small Bali village. It took place in the middle of the main square in the large *banjar* meeting hall with a towering sheet metal roof. The program was scheduled to begin at 11 a.m., but the guest *gamelan* groups arrived late on their flatbed trucks as the audience slowly filtered in.

It wasn't until 1 p.m. that finally Bob Brown, his deep baritone voice perfectly suited to his stout stature, greeted the audience and introduced the first group, the ethereal iron *gamelan selonding* from the primitive *Bali Aga* village of Tengganan. A priest appeared onstage, lit incense, sprinkled holy water and prayed to sanctify the occasion, and the *gamelan* proceeded to play.

The audience in the large hall was made up mostly of Westerners, tourists and performers. Judy Slattum brought her tour group, and a few of our mutual American friends. The front few rows were occupied by the village notables and official guests. The villagers, however, seemed too timid to come inside and find seats. Instead, they peeked over the low wall that surrounded the hall, watching curiously.

The performance was dedicated to the legacy of Colin

McPhee, the noted musician and ethnomusicologist who had made Bali his home in the '30s. The afternoon program featured the original *gamelan*s with which McPhee had performed and composed. They were some of the very best in Bali and included the famed *Gamelan Semar Pegulingan* from Teges and the *Gamelan Angklung* from Sayan, where McPhee had built his home overlooking the spectacular Ayung River gorge.

For most of the day I sat enraptured, listening, writing in my journal and anticipating my own performance that night. Finally, around 6 p.m., it was time for the Flower Mountain Center students to perform along with our Balinese masters. The hall was now close to being filled with Westerners and even some adventurous villagers.

First off, the student *gamelan* under Pak Sumandhi with me on *ceng-ceng* played the richly textured "Golden Rain" piece that reverberated against the high metal roof exactly like rain. Next came Wenten's *"Titi Alit."* The audience loved it. Balinese were applauding enthusiastically who had probably never heard Western instruments much less an avant-garde, East-West fusion piece of music...

Pak Wenten has built "little bridges" of notes
so that we can cross over in harmony
from East to West, West to East.

Following our performance, the program truly lived up to being a world music festival. It featured African dance by the group of talented, young student-dancers from Cal Arts College and a Middle Eastern drumming and instrumental ensemble. It went on till nearly midnight. Many people stayed to the very end and showed their appreciation with a standing ovation. The first World Music Festival of Payangan was a huge success!

***

Our final days in Bali saw the dismantling of our old rice barn on the middle terrace and its reconstruction down on the lower terrace, overlooking the rice fields. Typical of how nothing goes to waste in Bali, a neighboring farmer took away the old thatch roof, which made it easier to move, but the floor and support posts must have weighed a ton!

I wanted to help carry the platform down to the lower terrace. Surya may have been afraid I would hurt myself. He took advantage of a two-day trip Judy and I took to the beach at Candi Dasa with Judy S. and her tour group to perform the herculean task. We returned to find the platform in place. According to Surya, it had taken six men three hours to struggle with the load down the ten terrace steps, one at a time. I joked that I could have done it single-handedly, secretly grateful my back had been spared.

In the gray early morning light, we watched the workers, the short father and tall brother of our housegirl, Wayan, who came all the way from Bangli in northeast Bali, arrive. They trod softly, reverentially, across the dewy grass towards the unfinished *lumbung*, its thin wooden ribs outlined against the misty golden, rising sun. The men paused, contemplating the work they would accomplish that day, before they slowly descended the wide, curving stone steps to the lower terrace to work.

Next came the young village women...

A line of Balinese women,
with backs strong and straight as bamboo,

carry baskets of cement on their heads
a quarter of a mile in from the road,
laughing and chit-chatting as they go
as if they were strolling to market.

With the rice barn removed, a lovely, pastoral view of the open fields over the compound wall was opened up. And now, inside the compound, we had a clear view of the new *padmasana* shrine from our *joglo*.

***

On *purnama,* the full moon celebration, all over Bali many temple *odalan* birthday celebrations, marriages and family celebrations were taking place. I attended an *odalan* in the village of Tegallingah as a guest of Nyoman Sedana, who once again was performing a puppet play.

Three o'clock, the time set for his performance, came and went, as any ceremony couldn't start without the priest, who habitually arrived late. This was especially true on *purnama* with so many celebrations scheduled. Finally at six thirty, Sedana had to perform in the dark without a screen or an oil lamp while the worshippers crowded into the small inner temple enclosure to be blessed and pray...

The priest rings his bell,
our clasped hands rise with the full moon.
We chant Om Shanti
over the cries of warring gods and demons
who fill every corner of the crowded courtyard
and the universe.

We attended the annual kite festival on an enormous stretch of deserted, breezy beachfront near the airport from where we would soon be departing. Young men representing their *banjars* arrived from all over Bali to display their creations and compete in various categories. They unloaded the kites from flatbed trucks. Then, proceeded by raucous *gamelan beleganjur* processional bands, they carried their enormous dragon kites with tails over twenty yards long into the large open field fronting the beach. At a signal from their leader, the line of young men ran, shouting, holding the long tails over their heads until their kites were launched skyward...

> *I soar with the kites*
> *into the Bali skies...*
> *pray for transcendence.*

***

Only a few months after we returned to Santa Cruz, Bali experienced a great tragedy. A terrorist bombing in Kuta took more than two hundred lives and injured many, destroying property and the livelihood of many Balinese families. Within weeks of the bombing, we joined the many Bali supporters in our community to put on a successful benefit and raised over $11,000 for disaster relief. Meanwhile, Bali tourism plummeted 80% immediately after the bombing and since has been very slow to recover. Their livelihoods related directly or indirectly to the tourist industry, nearly every Balinese family was adversely affected.

In spring of 2003 at our annual UCSC *gamelan* concert, we played and sang a piece written especially for our *gamelan* in support of Bali by our beloved friend and teacher, I Nyoman Wenten, called *Sami Gita* or "Song of Peace"...

Ngiring mangkin sare sinamian
Let us all come together

Sami Gita gemuruh kadi tatit
Let us all spread peace like thunder

Winangun Padma Puspita
To rebuild the Floating Lotus*

Hyong Wisesa nyarin jagat.
The Supreme Deity shines on all the world

We had no doubt that the Balinese way of life would survive and flourish once again. We all agreed that we must not abandon Bali and allow the terrorists to accomplish their evil goal of wrecking the economy.

I made a personal vow to return next year. It was the least I could do. After all, Bali had helped me accept what I couldn't change, brought me closer to those I loved and enabled me to become a better human being. Little did I know my next trip would allow me the opportunity to repay the Balinese for what they had done for me, and, at the same time, give me one of my greatest artistic triumphs.

* A metaphorical name for Bali.

VII
TOWARDS SPIRITUAL TRANSFORMATION
Seventh Trip—June 17 through July 15, 2003

A ll winter and spring of 2003, Judy worked on getting her art studio built in the backyard. By summer it was finished, and she was more than happy to stay put and paint while I made the pilgrimage to Bali alone. This would be the first time in forty-one years of marriage we would be apart for more than a week...

What a delicious agony
to miss my sweet wife
and devote myself instead
to my two mistresses,
writing and music.

I couldn't wait to immerse myself in the arts. I took my clarinet, Balinese flute and unfinished Bali manuscript to work on. I looked forward to performing once again at Flower Mountain World Music Center, though regrettably Pak Wenten would not be coming to Bali this summer.

The SARS travel ban was lifted just before I left, but just to be on the safe side, I brought along a mask. Entering the plane, I was relieved to see no one wearing one...

On Fathers' Day 2003,
at the open plane door,
I flirt with a stewardess
young enough to be my daughter
and leave my fears behind.

Of course, there were signs of the effects of 9/11 and SARS everywhere. Airport security in San Francisco was tight. I had to remove my shoes at the security gate and got frisked twice. Moving through the gate into Singapore airport, I anxiously glanced at my infra-red image on the video monitor as each passing person's temperature was instantly tested. The usually bustling terminal was abnormally quiet. Discount and sale signs were posted in the windows of the shops. At the Bali airport, I claimed my luggage to find the lock broken and an inspection notice atop the ruffled contents.

***

As I hauled my luggage through the compound gate, I was more warmly welcomed by Agus and Nyoman than ever before. We hadn't had any guests since the Kuta disaster the previous October.

We took our usual walk around the compound to see the latest improvements, including the new pond filled with carp where the rice barn had formerly been, and the new stone enclosure for the gleaming, white stone *padmasana.*

I commiserated with them about the tragic Kuta bombing. Both Agus and Nyoman expressed their gratitude that I had made the trip. I reassured them that nothing could keep me from coming to help support the Balinese people in their recovery.

They told me the Balinese Hindus accepted the Kuta disaster as the consequence of the world passing through the *kali yuga* "time of destruction" at the end of the last 2000-year cycle before another cycle of creation begins...

I come during Kali Yuga
to be with the Balinese,
feel their pain,
make their healing, mine.

There were no reprisals against the Muslim population in Bali. Immediately after the Kuta bombing, instead of blaming and wreaking revenge on the terrorists, the Balinese asked what evil they had done to bring this disaster on themselves. There was a heightened awareness of their overinvestment in tourism at the expense of the health, safety and welfare of their own people. Also, they were chagrined over the loss of the tourists' life and property because of the lack of sufficient safeguards.

Purification rituals took place all over the island along with much discussion and planning to keep this from ever happening again. Agus joked that these ceremonies all over the island were so powerful, most of the terrorists had been put into trance and rendered completely unable to escape. They had simply been rounded up in Java and brought to justice.

Two days later on the Balinese holiday of *Galungan*, Surya went down to Denpasar to help decorate his family compound and make preparations for the celebration. After his father's death, his mother continued to live there with her son, Nyoman and his family and single brother Gedé. Surya brought her back to our home to visit...

With great care, Surya's mother
places the offering on the white stone padmasana
draped with yellow cloth specially for Galungan.
She asks God to bless and protect our compound
surrounded by a world where there is little peace.

***

I returned to Flower Mountain where I played flute in the *gamelan* ensemble with Pak Terip. He made the long trip down from Munduk every day, yet he never seemed to be tired or out of sorts. Terip taught in the old traditional way of incremental repetition without a word being spoken. We'd practice a phrase over and over until he'd stop. Then he'd cock his head to one side, listening to his memory, and teach us a new one. His dedication was inspiring.

I reunited with Nyoman Sedana and his family at the *Pesta Kesenian* or Bali Arts Festival and spent the day with them. Pak I Wayan Rai, whom I hadn't seen in five years and was now president of STSI arts college, had personally invited me to participate in the Bali Arts Festival on the special night reserved for foreign guest performers.

What an honor! I asked Sedana to collaborate with me on an original composition to help support the Balinese in their recovery from the Kuta disaster. He invited me to stay the night with his family in Denpasar so we could start work on the new piece right away, since we only had a few weeks before our performance. Since I had last visited, his modest concrete three-room bungalow had been remodeled and was now a five-room palace surrounded by crenelated walls and a fancy, wrought-iron gate suitable for a Balinese prince.

The next day, we attended a special jazz concert given by an American group, the Bill Head Trio from New York. There

Pak Rai welcomed me and said it was a pleasure to have me take part in the festival as a friend and as a musician accomplished in both Balinese and Western music. Rai ushered me to one of the luxurious, plush-cushioned and carved front row seats reserved for dignitaries, right next to the jolly vice-governor of Bali! After some half-hearted attempts at communication, as the jazz trio played a Cole Porter tune, I quipped that it was too hot in Bali to make love "Night and Day," and we had a good laugh.

The next day, at the behest of Pak Rai, I sat in with the Bill Head Trio to demonstrate jazz improvisation at a special session for STSI music students...

Sweet Georgia Brown sounds
even sweeter and hotter
in a stuffy auditorium filled
with smiling Balinese students.

Class over, Nyoman and I went to lunch at a local *warung* then back to his house on the outskirts of Denpasar. While he went back to work at the college, I took a nap. After I got up, I went into Nyoman's study and began playing on the ten keys of his *gender* instrument to find a suitable mode that would be in tune with my clarinet. By the time Nyoman returned, I had composed a little melody, and we worked on a *kotekan*, the rhythmically interlocking lines two *gender* could play as accompaniment...

Sweating in the afternoon heat,
I let the notes of a new composition
wash over me, bring me cool peace.

This peace would be short lived as I would have to commute daily for the next few weeks between Lod Tunduh, Payangan and Denpasar. However, when I returned to Payangan the next day, I found first to my disappointment and then my relief that Pak Terip's *gamelan* group had been discontinued. The students were too busy with other musical commitments. No longer participating at Payangan, I was free to devote all my energies to developing and rehearsing the Bali Arts Festival piece.

Inspired by Pak Wenten's paean to Bali, I wrote words to the melody and a title, "Bali Spirit." Nyoman supplied me with the Balinese translation, as we planned to have the piece sung in both languages...

Let's come together and sing this song
Ngiring sameton magending

To Bali spirit that never dies
Jiwa Bali mangda nyangsan limbak

Let our love bring peace and joy forever more.
Tresna si-he anggen nyujur rahajeng.

In Denpasar a few days later, Pak Rai hosted a luncheon at a local restaurant for the foreign guests from the U.S., Canada and Japan who would be performing on the night of July 12th. There I met a classical violinist, also by the name of Bob Brown, who had a home in Ubud. I asked him to join Sedana and our group, and he enthusiastically accepted. At the lunch was Kathy Foley, a professor whom I knew from Santa Cruz, who was staying with Sedana's family while traveling on a Fullbright through Indonesia. I asked her to join us. She could sing the hymn part of the piece together with a very talented girl from England who was scheduled to play flute with two other groups. Meanwhile, Sedana had recruited a fine American student by the name of Andy McGraw from Wesleyan University. Andy brought in a drummer from Java to complete our ensemble.

I worked out some variations to the melody for the violin and clarinet and planned an improvisational section where Bob and I would solo to the accompaniment of the *gender.* I was exhilarated by the challenge of composing and performing a piece for five instruments and two voices that would be performed at a world-renowned festival!

We had little time to rehearse, arriving at the day of the performance after only a handful of run-throughs...

For a few moments in time,
East and West have come together
Balinese gender, Javanese drums
Western clarinet, violin and voices
in a hymn to one world!

At the close of the evening, Pak Rai called onstage all the foreign guest performers to take bows and receive the applause of the appreciative audience that included Judy S., Surya, Surya's family and friends. The stout, jolly vice-governor of Bali, whom I had met at the jazz concert, presented each of us with a specially inscribed silver plaque commemorating our performance. Smiling and nodding as he shook my hand and handed me the plaque, he said what sounded to me like *"Geh, geh!"* Without hesitation, I responded with a nod, smile and an answering *"Geh, geh!"*

At the celebratory dinner under a tent on the Art Center grounds, I expressed my gratitude to Pak Rai. He reminded me how pleased he had been to visit Santa Cruz nearly ten years ago, staying with Judy and I while he taught and performed with our *gamelan*. In return for his personal instruction on the flute, I gave him the benefit of what I knew about jazz improvisation. At that time, he promised he would return the favor someday, and now he had. As we clasped each other in friendship and said our goodbyes in the parking lot where my van was waiting, once again I thanked Pak Rai for inviting me and Pak Sedana, my dear friend, for collaborating. I told them both how much this performance had meant to me.

For days afterwards, I found it hard to accept what I had accomplished. I would go over the performance in my mind, painfully aware of how much better it could have been with more rehearsals, more care. Still, the energy and spirit were there and the audience applause and the performers enjoyment attested to a success.

I made the transition from teaching to a new, artistic life with confidence in my ability and became a more compassionate human being as a result. Now my real work would begin…

Bali has brought me
to the end of this book
and the beginning
of my spiritual transformation.